IMPLEMENTING STUDENT-LED CONFERENCES

EXPERTS IN ASSESSMENT™

SERIES EDITORS
THOMAS R. GUSKEY AND ROBERT J. MARZANO

Please call our toll-free number (800–818–7243)
or visit our website (www.corwinpress.com)
to order individual titles or the entire series.

IMPLEMENTING STUDENT-LED CONFERENCES

JANE M. BAILEY
THOMAS R. GUSKEY

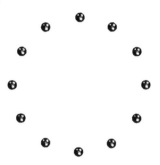

EXPERTS IN ASSESSMENT™

SERIES EDITORS
THOMAS R. GUSKEY AND ROBERT J. MARZANO

CORWIN PRESS, INC.
A Sage Publications Company
Thousand Oaks, California

For information:

 Corwin Press, Inc.
A Sage Publications Company
2455 Teller Road
Thousand Oaks, California 91320
E-mail: order@corwinpress.com

Sage Publications Ltd.
6 Bonhill Street
London EC2A 4PU
United Kingdom

Sage Publications India Pvt. Ltd.
M-32 Market
Greater Kailash I
New Delhi 110 048 India

Printed in the United States of America

Library of Congress Cataloging-in-Publication Data

Bailey, Jane M., 1953–
    Implementing student-led conferences / by Jane M. Bailey and Thomas R. Guskey.
        p. cm. — (Experts in assessment kit)
Includes bibliographical references and index.
    ISBN 0-8039-6855-8 (cloth: alk. paper)
    ISBN 0-8039-6856-6 (pbk: alk. paper)
  1. Student-led parent conferences. 2. Portfolios in education
I. Guskey, Thomas R.   II. Title.   III. Series.
    LC225.5 .B25 2000
    371.3'7—dc21   00-008784

This book is printed on acid-free paper.

                        05   10   9   8   7   6   5   4   3

Corwin Editorial Assistant: Catherine Kantor
Production Editor: Nevair Kabakian
Editorial Assistant: Candice Crosetti
Typesetter/Designer: Rebecca Evans
Cover Designer: Tracy E. Miller

Contents

Series Editors' Introduction

Standards, assessment, accountability, and grading—these are the issues that dominated discussions of education in the 1990s. Today, they are at the center of every modern education reform effort. As educators turn to the task of implementing these reforms, they face a complex array of questions and concerns that little in their background or previous experience has prepared them to address. This series is designed to help in that challenging task.

In selecting the authors, we went to individuals recognized as true experts in the field. The ideas of these scholar-practitioners have already helped shape current discussions of standards, assessment, accountability, and grading. But equally important, their work reflects a deep understanding of the complexities involved in implementation. As they developed their books for this series, we asked them to extend their thinking, to push the edge, and to present new perspectives on what should be done and how to do it. That is precisely what they did. The books they crafted provide not only cutting-edge perspectives but also practical guidelines for successful implementation.

We have several goals for this series. First, that it be used by teachers, school leaders, policy makers, government officials, and all those concerned with these crucial aspects of education reform. Second, that it helps broaden understanding of the complex issues involved in standards, assessment, accountability, and grading. Third, that it leads to more thoughtful policies and programs. Fourth, and most important, that it helps accomplish the basic goal for which all reform initiatives are intended—namely, to enable all students to learn excellently and to gain the many positive benefits of that success.

— *Thomas R. Guskey*
Robert J. Marzano
Series Editors

Preface

Communicating to parents what their children have been working on in school and what learning progress they have made is one of a teacher's most challenging responsibilities. In most cases, however, new teachers have scant knowledge and little training on how to meet this challenge. The following "author's reflection" best describes how we came to see the value in having students lead their own conferences as an effective means for reporting student learning to parents.

As a first-year high school teacher on parent conference night, I remember arriving early, armed with my grade book, sharpened pencils and student folders. As I opened the steel door to the gymnasium, I heard the "clunk" of a heavy switch and then the low buzz of big mercury vapor lights warming up. Under that dull, bluish light, I found my seat in the middle row of a sea of small desks lined up on the gym floor. Facing me were two straight rows of metal folding chairs. On either side of me were long rows of teacher stations identical to mine. As I arranged my materials, 60 other teachers filtered into the gymnasium, searching for the small table sign with his or her name indicating a temporary "office" location for the evening. As the big lights grew brighter and brighter, I wondered how long this evening would last.

At the appointed hour, all six gymnasium doors opened and a small army of parents rushed in, vying to be first in line to pick up their child's report card and to speak with the teachers. Some, I noticed, picked up the report card and left the gymnasium as quickly as possible. Others fought to sit in the first chair opposite the "toughest" social studies teacher in the school, whose line was 12 parents deep within the first 5 minutes of scheduled conference time. Some couples arrived together, studied one or more report cards, and planned a "divide and conquer" strategy in order to see all 18 of the teachers for their three high school-age children.

Soon, all I heard were voices rising to be heard, the sound of metal chairs scraping across the floor, the constant "clunk" of big doors opening and closing, and the dull buzz of warm mercury vapor lights. I looked at the small line of parents waiting to see me and thought of my students. I taught ninth-grade

"Basic English" classes. Although they were in high school, most of my students had failed to learn to read and write properly. They had low self-esteem and many lacked any sense of responsibility. They stood out from their classmates by accumulating the most discipline referrals, attendance concerns, and "attitude" problems in the school. I needed to see all of their parents. Instead, I saw mostly those whose children were compliant and hardworking. I found myself wishing that students were present to hear my compliments and/or my concerns. I kept thinking, "Why am I telling Mom or Dad all of these things when I could be talking with the person who is responsible for this work—the student?" I knew that once parents reached home, most of what I said would be lost in the translation.

So, each fall and spring, I left the big gymnasium after scheduled parent conference times feeling more and more uncomfortable and wondering how I could possibly make a difference in this whole experience of parent-teacher conferences. I thought about the impersonal setting in that high school gym with noise and a lack of privacy for parents. I was troubled by the lack of student responsibility in the grading and evaluation process. At times, I felt that I did not have enough reliable information collected to really justify the grades I was assigning. All in all, I began to dread the whole experience.

Since those early years as a classroom teacher in both general and special education, I have served as a high school principal, a regional service agency consultant, and a district curriculum coordinator. Throughout these experiences, questions regarding how to increase parent involvement and student responsibility continued to surface. In the early 1990s, while reading and researching information on portfolio assessment for a teacher training project I was leading, I stumbled across a concept then new to me: student-led conferences. I had heard an elementary teacher from a neighboring district talk about the concept in a university course I was taking and decided to do a literature search on the topic. Although only a handful of articles came up in that search, one was especially helpful. This article, titled "Student-Led Parent-Teacher Conferences," was written by Nancy Little and John Allan (1989). It described a method for organizing conferences with parents that were led by students. The classroom teacher met with each family group only to facilitate and to offer brief comments on student performance. The students were responsible for leading parents through a discussion of student work collected over time and organized into a portfolio. Suddenly, I saw the tool for addressing my nagging concerns.

Definition of Student-Led Conferences

The term *student-led conference* is almost self-explanatory. A student-led conference is a conference with parents led by the student. The classroom teacher's role becomes that of a facilitator. In a student-led conference, students lead parents through a discussion of their work, which is usually organized in a portfolio collection. Typically, several conferences are conducted simultaneously in a classroom with family groups seated far enough apart to allow privacy. The teacher (or teachers) circulates among family groups, stopping long enough to make pertinent comments and answer any questions. Students primarily direct the conversation, which is focused on their work and classroom behavior.

Effectiveness of Student-Led Conferences

The real power in this innovation is that student-led conferences require *students* to take most of the responsibility for reporting what they have learned. To prepare for this responsibility, students must evaluate and reflect upon their work on a regular basis. They must organize their work into a thoughtful collection (a portfolio), and they must organize their thoughts about learning well enough to articulate those thoughts to others. In short, students must be actively involved in the process of learning.

In addition, student-led conferences are an effective method for promoting parent participation in the learning process. Many schools that have implemented student-led conferences have seen a dramatic increase in parent attendance at conferences. Based on the procedures described in Little and Allan's work, we helped guide a small group of 13 teachers from all different grade levels in implementing student-led conferences. Evaluations of these conferences involving surveys administered to both teachers and parents yielded impressive results. Data showed the average parent participation rate across school buildings was 95%, with one elementary building reporting 100% participation from parents or family members.

Further, from interviews we have conducted, it is clear that individual teachers at many different grade levels like student-led conferences as a way of promoting student responsibility and parent involvement. Teachers consistently report to us that student-led conferences are an easy concept for everyone to understand. They also say that the preparation does not require an inordinate amount of instructional time and blends well into the regular classroom routine. In addition, many teachers have reported that student-led conferences are a more efficient way to meet and talk with parents of *all* students in a classroom. Teachers we interviewed overwhelmingly reported that they felt very positive about the success of this type of conference, and all said they will continue student-led conferences as a classroom practice.

Teacher evaluations from our original pilot group were so positive that with the support of the local educational service agency, we produced a video that chronicles their experiences in implementing student-led conferences. Since the video was produced, all 11 local school districts within the service area have implemented student-led conferences in some form, and several buildings now use student-led conferences each spring.

In addition, parent surveys from this group were very positive. One parent said, "I didn't know my son could speak so well about his work. He really does know what he is doing!" Another parent wrote, "My daughter struggles with self-esteem. She was very nervous prior to the conference, and I was very nervous for her. When we got to the conference, though, and she began telling me about her work, she just blossomed. Thank you so much for giving her this experience. It has changed her!" Parent comments validated teacher perceptions about the success of the conferences. All parents who returned surveys suggested that the practice continue.

Elementary schools were the first to embrace the concept of student-led conferences because scheduling is somewhat easier than in secondary schools. However, in recent years, we have had great success in middle and high schools as well. Today, we are beginning to look at student-led conferences from a district-wide perspective. We are beginning to talk about ways in which we can enrich and deepen the student-led conference experience for students through increased reflection and responsibility as they progress through the grades.

How the Book Is Organized

We have organized the book around a set of practical issues involved in implementing student-led conferences. Chapter 1 focuses on the purpose of having students lead a conference. Given a clear purpose and philosophy, Chapter 2 discusses the changes in roles and responsibilities necessary for a successful student-led conference experience. Chapter 3 discusses in greater detail what a student-led conference "looks like" and outlines some variations in format, such as student-involved conferences and presentation conferences. Chapters 4, 5, and 6 get into the actual logistics of preparation, organization, and scheduling. Chapter 7 includes suggestions from classroom teachers on how to anticipate possible problems or difficult situations and prepare accordingly. Chapter 8 suggests some methods for measuring the success of student-led conferences and for processing the conference with students in order to extend learning. Finally, Chapter 9 summarizes the role of student-led conferences in authentic assessment and reporting. Throughout the book, we have included helpful forms and organizers teachers have shared with us and invite readers to adapt these for their own use.

There are many different ways to configure a student-led conference experience to fit learning goals, time schedules, and different purposes for the conference. Throughout this book, we will describe different models teachers have used successfully. We have also included actual teacher stories to illustrate the strengths of different models of student-led conferences and to high-light what teachers have learned from the inevitable glitches that occur when implementing a new idea.

Our goal in writing this book is to help readers understand

- Why it is effective for students to lead a conference
- What an effective model for student-led conferences looks like
- How to prepare and organize for student-led conferences
- How to evaluate the effectiveness of student-led conferences

From this understanding, our hope is that readers will have the necessary in-formation to design and implement a system of student-led conferences that fits the context of a particular classroom or school.

In our work, we have come to realize that we must become more focused and intentional in developing a system for reporting student learning to par-ents and other significant audiences. We believe that student-led confer-ences, as part of a school-wide reporting system, can be used to report student progress to parents and others in a way that increases student responsibility. We invite teachers to consider this simple innovation as a way to encourage students to produce quality work and to communicate their work to others.

As educators, we have come a long way since those first parent confer-ences in the high school gymnasium. In particular, we have learned how to in-crease parent participation and student responsibility through involving stu-dents in conferences. This book is designed to help those interested in sharing in these experiences. We outline practical guidelines for successfully imple-menting student-led conferences in a variety of school environments. We also share detailed information on the successes and concerns of the teachers who have implemented student-led conferences. Our hope is that through sharing stories and information from many experienced teachers, parents, and stu-dents, you will find the tools necessary to design a system of student-led con-ferences that is successful in your classroom or school.

Acknowledgments

The authors wish to acknowledge the following teachers who contributed comments, stories, forms, or moral support during the preparation of this book. Their expertise and commitment to student success is an inspiration to us, and we thank them all for their time, their dedication, and their permission to share some of their best work. We appreciate them!

Betty Arnold
Charlevoix-Emmet Intermediate
    School District
Charlevoix, Michigan

Janine Bingham
Shay Elementary
Harbor Springs Public Schools
Harbor Springs, Michigan

Daniel Bower
Blackbird Elementary
Harbor Springs Public Schools
Harbor Springs, Michigan

Carolyn Downton
East Jordan Elementary School
East Jordan Public Schools
East Jordan, Michigan

Kelli Fenlon
Charlevoix-Emmet Intermediate
    School District
Charlevoix, Michigan

Patti Gabos
Charlevoix-Emmet Intermediate
    School District
Charlevoix, Michigan

Jill Haan
Sheridan Elementary School
Public Schools of Petoskey
Petoskey, Michigan

Teresa Noirot Hart
East Jordan Middle School
East Jordan Public Schools
East Jordan, Michigan

Stephanie Inman
East Jordan Elementary School
East Jordan Public Schools
East Jordan, Michigan

David Johnson
The Cooperative Learning Center
University of Minnesota
Minneapolis, Minnesota

Joyce Marquardt
Shay Elementary
Harbor Springs Public Schools
Harbor Springs, Michigan

Cathy Meyer-Looze
Petoskey High School
Public Schools of Petoskey
Petoskey, Michigan

Myra Munroe
Central Lake Elementary School
Central Lake Public Schools
Central Lake, Michigan

Shelly A. Potter
Independent Consultant
The Potter Press
Birmingham, Michigan

Denise Rice
Ottawa Elementary School
Public Schools of Petoskey
Petoskey, Michigan

Paul Ryder
Retired from Sheridan Elementary
Public Schools of Petoskey
Petoskey, Michigan

Kathy Stangis
East Jordan High School
East Jordan Public Schools
East Jordan, Michigan

About the Authors

Jane M. Bailey is the Curriculum and Staff Development Coordinator for the Public Schools of Petoskey in northern lower Michigan. In addition to providing district leadership in the areas of curriculum and staff development, she serves as special education and federal programs director. She has more than 20 years of experience in education in a variety of roles including teacher, special education consultant, high school principal, and staff development coordinator for a regional service agency. She is coauthor of a chapter titled "Reporting Achievement at the Secondary Level: What and How" in the 1996 *Yearbook* for the Association for Supervision and Curriculum Development (ASCD). She is on the executive board of the Michigan affiliate of the National Staff Development Council and consults with school districts in the areas of assessment, grading, and school improvement.

Thomas R. Guskey is Professor of Educational Policy Studies and Evaluation at the University of Kentucky. A graduate of the University of Chicago, he has taught at all levels, served as an administrator in Chicago Public Schools, and is the author/editor of nine books including *Implementing Mastery Learning, Improving Student Learning in College Classrooms, Communicating Student Learning,* and *Evaluating Professional Development.* He has won many awards for his work, including the National Staff Development Council's prestigious Article of the Year and Book of the Year awards. He is a frequent presenter at national conferences, was recently featured in a special segment on National Public Radio, and has worked with educators throughout the United States and Canada, as well as in Europe, Asia, and the Middle East.

To Tom and John

**CORWIN
PRESS**

The Corwin Press logo—a raven striding across an open book—represents the happy union of courage and learning. We are a professional-level publisher of books and journals for K–12 educators, and we are committed to creating and providing resources that embody these qualities. Corwin's motto is "Success for All Learners."

CHAPTER 1

Philosophy and Purpose of Student-Led Conferences

Early experiences such as the one in the high school gym described in the Preface led us to question the purpose and effectiveness of traditional parent-teacher conferences. As teachers, we assume that our purpose in conducting a conference is to communicate a student's progress toward meeting the goals or standards for each class or subject area. When we talk about students to their parents, however, we often feel that something is missing. We have difficulty conveying to parents all the fine points we want to share about students' work, about their participation in class, and about their success in meeting standards. We feel constrained by time, but more important, that we are not the ones who can most accurately report student progress. We realize the "something missing" is actually *someone* missing from this conversation: the student. For a discussion of student work to be relevant, accurate, and complete, students must be involved in some way. Having students lead a conference with parents or other significant adults is a way to maximize this involvement.

Personal experiences first led us to question conference formats, but other significant information on effective ways for reporting student learning (Guskey, 1996) has convinced us that student-led conferences promote three elements essential to improving student performance in school: relevance, responsibility, and reporting. These "3 Rs" form the philosophical base of student-led conferences.

Relevance: "Why Are We Doing This?"

This question is one that every teacher with more than a few weeks' experience has probably heard from students—and, it's a good one. Jacobs (1997) stresses that as teachers, we must begin to see the curriculum that is experienced by an individual student. We can no longer afford to teach only what we like to teach or what we know well. Instead, we must consider the experiences of individual students as they move through the curriculum from kindergarten through grade 12. From this student viewpoint, relevance takes on new meaning. In order for learning to be relevant, students must be able to see the importance of the concepts they are learning and must be able to connect those concepts to prior learning and to the world outside the classroom. In addition, students can more easily see relevance in their daily work when they know that an audience beyond the walls of the classroom will see and review this work.

It is also essential to understand how important a collection of student work becomes to children. Hebert (1998) notes,

> What we didn't know then [10 years ago] was that the process of selecting samples of one's own work and assembling them into a portfolio is profoundly important to children. We also learned that all children have a natural ability and desire to tell their story through the contents of the portfolio. Even now, we remain excited about capturing the individual voices of our students through portfolio collections. (p. 583)

The process of capturing the "individual voice" is what is exciting and relevant about using portfolio collections to report to parents or others. With a student-led conference, students are telling a story from their own perspective. Parents have the opportunity to really understand and appreciate from the student's point of view what learning has been significant and important. Given this type of reporting over time, parents have the opportunity to see the intellectual growth and development of their child from a new perspective. With more traditional conferences, growth is evaluated and reported solely from the teacher's perspective or through the teacher's lens. The teacher's perspective is an important one, of course, but it is not the only one parents need to know. The child's perspective is essential if parents are to fully understand and appreciate the relevance that learning experiences have for students. Hebert (1998) goes on to say, "The physical act of attaching meaning to a specific piece of work contributes significantly to the child's metacognitive growth" (p. 585). The process of reporting to parents through a student-led conference further strengthens meaning and relevance for students.

Responsibility: Making the Student More Responsible for Learning

An important question that teachers often ask is, "How can I get my students to be more responsible and do their best work?" A student-led conference offers one method for increasing student responsibility for learning. Because students know they will be reporting to parents or other significant adults on a range of topics over time, they begin to see the importance of completing work, keeping track of work, and making sure work is done well.

In order to prepare for student-led conferences, most teachers incorporate a regular system for helping students maintain a portfolio or collection of work. A portfolio may be primarily teacher-directed; that is, the teacher selects the standards or goals for student learning and decides what work *must* be included in the portfolio to show parents. Or, a portfolio may be primarily student-directed, whereby students decide which pieces of work best reflect classroom performance. We agree with Hebert (1998) that "the selection of contents of the portfolio is an evolving process shared by child and teachers" (p. 584). We have come to realize that the best collections of student work result from a combination of teacher direction and student selection. Students should have some choice in what work is included in the portfolio, and students should maintain and own the portfolio. Ownership and active involvement promote student responsibility and accountability.

For students to take on greater responsibility and be accountable for their work, they must see relevance. They must also value the work they are doing and must be actively engaged in managing their own learning. Glasser (1997), in describing choice theory, says "we are all driven by four psychological needs that are embedded in our genes: the need to belong, the need for power, the need for freedom, and the need for fun" (p. 599). Certainly, our observations of students in classrooms confirm that when students enjoy what they are doing, when they feel a sense of ownership and pride in their work, and when they are doing work "that matters," they will produce higher quality work. In Glasser's terms, when students are able to satisfy one or more of these four basic needs, they feel good. From written surveys following student-led conferences, we have found that students enjoy a sense of power or control over the situation. They feel important ("I realized that I didn't need my teacher to explain things to my parents. I know what I'm doing."). And, they have fun in the process ("I felt very smart and special.").

Another consequence of student-led conferences often described by students is that they provide the opportunity to learn something new. That is, the experience itself promotes new learning on the part of both student and adults. In this way, student-led conferences are like performance-based assessment in that students acquire new learning through the process of completing the assessment task (Mitchell & Neill, 1992). In preparing for a student-led conference, students must learn to describe their work. They must engage in self-reflection in order to articulate their thoughts about their work. By preparing and presenting the conference, students learn something important that is typically not an intentional part of the curriculum.

In *Understanding by Design*, Grant Wiggins and Jay McTighe (1998) describe six facets that make up what they call "understanding"; in other words, what it means to truly *understand* something. One of the facets they describe is "self-knowledge: the wisdom to know one's ignorance and how one's patterns of thought and action inform as well as prejudice understanding" (p. 57). They go on to suggest that to assess a student's level of self-knowledge, we must "require students to self-assess their past as well as their present work" (p. 97). Wiggins and McTighe point to the use of portfolios of student work as one common tool that teachers employ in order to ask students to review and assess their own work. Teachers pose questions such as, "How does your work show how you have improved? What task or assignment was the most challenging and why? Which selection are you most proud of and why?" (p. 97).

Throughout the process of preparing for and conducting student-led conferences, answering these and other questions engages students in thoughtful self-reflection. As Wiggins and McTighe (1998) suggest, it is also important to "assess for self-knowledge" (p. 97). That is, students need to realize what they do and *do not* understand about a given subject. With careful planning and guidance, a student-led conference can be a wonderful vehicle for encouraging students to examine their own knowledge on a subject.

Reporting to Parents and Others: Increasing Effectiveness

The question parents ask is, "How is my child doing?" Reporting student progress to parents or other significant adults has become increasingly important as educators are being asked to be accountable for student achievement results. Guskey (1996) notes in the introduction to *Communicating Student Learning*, "Few topics in education are more controversial than grading, reporting, and communicating student learning. Teachers, students, administrators, parents, and community members all agree that we need better reporting systems" (p. 1). We have come to see the student-led conference as one way to effectively communicate student learning to parents in a detailed and direct way. When students report directly to parents, information is communicated in a form everyone can understand and use. As learning becomes increasingly complex from kindergarten through high school, a portfolio collection becomes a comprehensive way to demonstrate student growth and progress over time. And, as described earlier, the actual conference is a learning experience and can certify where additional work is needed.

In our experience, student-led conferences may be conducted with or without a formal "report card." Teachers who have asked students to conduct conferences both with and without report cards indicate no strong preferences. In fact, teachers with whom we have worked report that parents who attend a student-led conference with the goal of picking up a report card often take only a cursory glance at the written report. They feel they learn much more about student progress from the actual conference. Parents have commented on written surveys that "the report card is OK, but I now know much more about what my child is doing each day in school and about what she is actually learning." Given the primary goal of *communication*, student-led conferences are an excellent way to communicate student achievement or performance.

Additional Reasons to Implement Student-Led Conferences

In addition to the "3 Rs" of relevance, responsibility, and reporting, student-led conferences provide an excellent incentive for increasing parent participation in schools. As mentioned in the Preface, a survey distributed in schools that have implemented student-led conferences indicates an average parent participation rate of 95%, with one elementary building at 100% parent participation. Prior to implementation of student-led conferences, average participation rates in the same buildings ranged from 65% to 90%.

Some schools have elected to implement a "portfolio night" instead of more traditional parent-teacher conferences. On portfolio night, students from all grade levels sit down for a short, informal conference with parents to explain what a portfolio is, how it is used in the classroom, and what type of work parents might expect to see at the end of the year. Some schools incorporate an ice cream social, pizza party for families, or other social event as part of portfolio night in order to encourage parent or family participation. Still other schools combine a portfolio night in the fall with a formally scheduled student-led conference in the spring to allow parents to review the portfolio collection over the year. Most schools find such activities increase parent participation dramatically.

Finally, we want to highlight one other important goal that student-led conferences may achieve: celebration. Hebert (1998) describes conferences led by students in her building as a "celebration of student competence . . . an opportunity for children to present their portfolios to their own parents" (p. 585). She goes on to say that "learning is worth celebrating, and children can be competent participants in that celebration" (p. 585). In Hebert's school, students participate in the production of a classroom videotape approximately 15 to 20 minutes long that is intended to portray a day in the life of a particular group of students. This includes the learning that takes place in special subject areas of art, music, physical education, Spanish, and computers. Many videotapes also include recess activities and selected field trips. What better way to celebrate student learning than having students write and produce their own film! We know that children value fun, and this type of experience can be great fun for all involved.

In closing, one teacher's story best illustrates *why* we would have students lead a conference.

> The preparation for student-led conferences is great. The work begins at the beginning of the year, talking about concepts like being self-directed, setting goals, reflecting, producing quality work, portfolios, and more. . . .
>
> We begin to save papers and reflect in September. We try to teach students to save quality work *and* work that could have been done better. We asked one student why he chose the paper he did (it was only half complete) and he replied he needed to show his parents how well he can do but that he needs to work faster. Taking ownership for what you can do well is easy, but when students start understanding what they need to improve—then they are learning.
>
> For one parent, the student-led conference was an eye-opening experience. The child lived with a large extended family and had very little one-to-one time with his mother. The pressure of supporting the family, the younger siblings, and being a single parent left little time for this 8-year-old. After an hour conference, this mother was totally impressed with how much her child knew about his education. She had never really sat down to talk to him about his education and the future, and this opened the door for further discussions.

This example illustrates the "3 Rs" of student-led conferences: relevance, responsibility, and reporting. Through student-led conferences, students begin to see why they are saving and reflecting upon their work (relevance). They also must take responsibility for creating a thoughtful collection of student work to share with their parents in a face-to-face conference (responsibility and reporting).

Throughout these pages, we invite readers to "open the door for further discussions" with colleagues, parents, and students through the implementation of student-led conferences.

CHAPTER **2**

Roles and Responsibilities of Participants

Successful student-led conferences require changes in the roles each participant has become accustomed to through traditional parent-teacher conferences. Teachers become facilitators while students become leaders. Parents become active listeners and questioners. Support personnel such as secretaries, teaching assistants, and administrators become active participants in the preparation and implementation of conferences. Following is a description of the new roles and responsibilities for all those involved in successfully implementing student-led conferences.

The Teacher's Role

As novice teachers, we used to think we had to have "all the answers" and that we were responsible for all or most of the learning that occurs in the classroom. Our role was "wise one" and our responsibility, as we saw it, was to impart knowledge to students. We organized the learning environment and reported progress from one perspective: our own. We were serious, intentional, committed, and hard-working. Sooner or later, most of us realized that *we* were working harder than our students—and probably learning more!

Struggling with the issue of student responsibility, we began to see that in order to help students become more responsible, we needed to give up some of our control—that is, we needed to shift the focus to students taking more responsibility for their own learning. Student-led conferences are a simple and effective tool for accomplishing this shift.

So, how does the teacher's role change with a student-led conference? One comment from a teacher implementing student-led conferences is especially relevant to the teacher's role and responsibilities. Asked to describe her first experience with student-led conferences, this fifth-grade teacher wrote,

My overall reaction went from, "Why am I doing this?" to, "Is there any other way!" I was very nervous just before conferences. I knew what I wanted the kids to do . . . but could they pull it off? They went above and beyond any of my expectations. They were professional and took this very seriously.

I did have a time of depression during the first few conferences: I wasn't needed. I didn't know where to go or what to do with myself. I would walk by a conference and they would stop talking! So, I stayed away. By the end of the day, I accepted that I wasn't in charge, and I was getting paid for all the pre-conference work!

As this teacher quickly discovered, she became a facilitator as students led their parents through a discussion about their progress and learning. The teacher's responsibility in this process is primarily to organize the conference environment to guarantee success. This includes scheduling, guiding portfolio collection, rehearsing with students, and arranging classroom space to accommodate families. Then the teacher steps back and lets the students conduct conferences. Students become the leaders; the teacher becomes a guide, an observer, an unobtrusive helper. One kindergarten teacher's comment also illustrates this role change: "I was so proud of the children showing their parents their work . . . such a positive experience for the children and a relaxing time for me!" A first-grade teacher wrote, "I've never worked so hard preparing for conferences in my entire 15 years of teaching . . . [but] Wow! I was so impressed with the way the kids handled themselves. Just think how much better their self-evaluation skills will get through the years."

The Student's Role

Of course, the student's role also changes dramatically from that of a non-participant or a passive observer to one of leader. Throughout all stages of a student-led conference—preparation, implementation, and evaluation—the student is the key person. The student becomes responsible for working with teachers to identify strengths and learning needs and then for collecting evidence over time to illustrate progress. In addition, the student takes an active role in helping with many of the details of the actual conference: inviting parents and scheduling, role-playing and rehearsing, preparing the physical space for family seating, and taking home pertinent information for parents both before and after the conference.

Student reflection is an additional and important dimension of the student's role and responsibility. In a traditional report to parents through a parent-teacher meeting, student reflection is missing. At best, teachers and parents try to make informed guesses about student reasoning or motivation.

When students know they must be ready to talk about their work to parents, teachers, or other significant adults, they naturally engage in self-reflection. They must ask themselves questions such as, "Why am I choosing this piece of work? How can I best show my parents how I behave in class? What *do* I need to work on and improve? What are my future goals?" And, in some cases, questions arise such as, "Where did I put my math papers?" Or, "Why didn't I take this work more seriously? Why did I hurry so much?" Getting students to verbalize or to write about their choices in a collection of work is a powerful tool to promote metacognition and self-awareness.

Student self-evaluation is one other important component of any student-led conference. Students write or talk with teachers about their perceptions of the conference and make suggestions for future improvements. Teachers often help students extend learning by taking the time for evaluation activities. The following responses are typical of those from students when asked to complete a sentence that began, "One thing I learned *about myself* during this conference was":

> "... now I know how to speak to other people without getting embarrassed."

> "... that I have to eat breakfast!"

> "... I do a very nice job."

> "... I was a better student than I thought."

> "... I'm a lot braver than I thought."

> "... I am capable of doing conferences without my teacher."

> "... I've got a lot of talents. I didn't know it!"

When asked to complete the sentence, "Something I think *my parent(s)* learned about me during this conference was ...," students responded with answers like

> "... that I'm very confident and determined."

> "... I'm a good student."

> "... that I am capable of doing things teachers do."

> "... that I have improved over time."

... and our personal favorite:

> "... that I'm definitely not perfect!"

Students at all grade levels, kindergarten through high school, repeatedly report increased confidence and pride, and actually, some amount of surprise in their ability to explain their work, to set goals, and to express their attitudes about school and learning to their parents or other significant adults. As students take on the role of leader, they begin to see the direct connection between their own efforts and responsibility and their success in the classroom.

The Parent's Role

Parents truly become partners in learning when students lead a conference. Student comments consistently point to the importance of having parents care and inquire about classroom work. We find that when students have a meaningful audience in addition to the classroom teacher, their work takes on increased importance and relevance. Students of all ages enjoy showing their work, talking about their accomplishments, answering questions, and receiving attention for their efforts. In a student-led conference, parents or other adults provide reinforcement, encouragement, and praise. They also ask probing questions, help students look realistically at the quality of their work, and facilitate deeper student self-reflection.

Parents consistently comment that having one-to-one time with their children is a very valuable part of the conference experience. One parent wrote, "I spent time with my son. I don't get to do much of that." The parent of a fourth grader commented, "Paul had to listen to the concerns and suggestions that I had about his studies. When confronting him at home, he seemed not to care as much. I also liked seeing the work *he* felt was really his best." Parents say that, typically, discussions at home are centered around the weekly folder of work that is sent home or the messy bunch of papers that sporadically fly out of a backpack. Parents report that in this type of conference, held in a "business-like" setting, their children take the discussion of student work very seriously.

An elementary teacher who regularly conducts student-led conferences described one family of a fifth grader who spent more than an hour discussing long-term goals for high school and college until she politely reminded them of the late evening hour. The teacher was reluctant to stop this conference. She reported,

> I never would have expected this child to have such a serious conversation with his parents. I also never thought this child was interested enough in his work to really be thinking about college. Because all of the other families had gone home, I felt like a bit of an eavesdropper, but the conversation I heard was so moving, I just couldn't cut the conference short. This confirmed for me the importance of having students really talk with their parents about their work and their goals.

Finally, the parents' role in a student-led conference is to listen. Said one parent, "My son was quick to remind me that this was a *student*-led conference!"

Another parent, concerned that her daughter had difficulty with self-esteem, wrote,

> I expected her to be nervous and uncomfortable, but she was confident and well-prepared. During the conference, she identified her strengths, didn't dwell on weaknesses. Conducting the conference seemed to give her confidence and I saw pride and maturity that is so rarely demonstrated by her. . . . After the conference, it was obvious she felt successful and very proud—justifiably so.

Another parent wrote, "My child showed maturity, responsibility and pride. It was nice to learn about her schooling through *her.* A parent can really see what school is like through the eyes of the child."

We need to be able to see what school is like through the eyes of children in order to improve instruction and encourage higher student achievement. By listening and evaluating student work through a student-led conference, teachers and parents can learn a great deal about how to help individual students succeed and excel.

The Role of Administrators and Office Staff

The role of administrators and office staff in implementing student-led conferences is an essential one. They help by encouraging innovation, facilitating scheduling, and by providing the time and training necessary for teachers to learn about the concept and to organize well for conferences.

The building principal can help educate parents about student-led conferences through organizing parent information nights, writing short articles in the school newsletter or local newspaper, sending letters home explaining the concept, and talking with staff about how best to organize for success. The building principal can also review student work in preparation for conferences. One building principal we know uses Post-it™ notes to make comments on the work in student portfolios. In this way, the principal provides students with an audience beyond the classroom, which is very motivating to some students. This type of involvement also helps the building principal connect with students in very positive and meaningful ways.

School secretaries and counselors are key people in helping teachers schedule student-led conferences. Schools that implement this type of conference building-wide have some unique scheduling concerns. Parents who have two, three, or four children in one building need special scheduling consideration. Also, parents who may be unavailable during scheduled conference times may need special appointments. The school secretary and/or counselor can help schedule families appropriately. In addition, office support may be needed in sending invitations home or publicizing the conferences successfully. In any school, the secretary is often the first line of defense when parents have questions or concerns, so it is important the office staff be well informed and ready to answer questions or refer parents to appropriate staff.

School counselors, in addition to supporting teachers through scheduling and preparation, need to be available to parents who have concerns during or after the conference. In fact, counselors may join a student-led conference to help answer questions about school services or to assist students with future planning and goal-setting. School counselors need to be visible and available while conferences are conducted.

Finally, principals, office staff, or counselors can all be a major help in preparing students for conferences through role-playing. In Chapter 4, we discuss the importance of having students rehearse for a student-led conference. All available adults in the school, including cooks and custodians, are valuable as "parents" in a role-playing situation.

The Role of Co-Curricular or Support Teachers

Art, music, physical education, special education, and other areas are important parts of a student's education. Sometimes, these areas are not afforded the same importance in scheduling conferences as the "core" areas: math, science, language arts, and social studies. Yet, art, music, and physical education teachers are often leaders in designing portfolios, planning exhibits and performances of student work, and promoting student self-evaluation. Their guidance can help students create a collection of work that encompasses a broad, rich perspective on each student's strengths and learning challenges.

Co-curricular or support teachers make sure that student work is added to the portfolio. This becomes a challenge with subjects such as art, music, and physical education. In many schools, art teachers help students create visual displays in halls or in an art room so that parents may visit the display with their child as part of the regular conference. Being experts in design, art teachers can also help students design a unique and individual portfolio container. Students at all grade levels enjoy creating their own portfolio cover, box, or other storage device. We have seen everything from pizza or cereal boxes to metal hinged books to hold student work. Portfolio collections are enhanced when art teachers help students convey messages visually.

We find that video- or audio tapes are an excellent way for students to show their progress in music or physical education. Many teachers now build time into the student-led conference schedule to allow use of a VCR and monitor or audio cassette player for reviewing student performances in co-curricular areas. Art, music, and physical education teachers need to be involved in student-led conferences as much as the schedule will allow. Samples of student work in these areas provide an important piece of the puzzle in reporting student learning.

Two high school teachers have begun a successful collaboration that involves the use of technology in student-led conferences. A ninth-grade humanities teacher requires her students to write several essays and create projects related to history and language arts concepts. Her partner, a business services and technology teacher, helps students keep an electronic portfolio and create presentations to display portfolio contents to parents. Their student-led conferences are held in the computer lab with four or five families at a time gathered around a computer monitor or video projector to view student work.

Special education teachers help students prepare and collect the type of work samples that show progress toward Individualized Educational Plan (IEP) goals. One special education teacher wrote about her experiences in trying student-led conferences for the first time in her school:

> As we planned for implementation in a fourth-grade classroom with two other teachers, we had a conversation about how to prepare the students with special needs. As a learning disabilities specialist, I offered to "push in" to help any student that may need it. . . . We chose work to discuss with parents, organized the portfolio, reflected on work samples, and role-played the conference. All of the students performed at a level that surprised us. All of the students led a conference. The students with special needs performed just as well as any other student. Our only adaptation was to provide more coaching during the preparation phase.

Special education teachers are also valuable resource people for finding ways to promote student self-reflection and goal-setting, because they are experts in diagnosing learning problems and designing ways to address those problems. This same special education teacher, reflecting on student-led conferences, wrote,

> We came to the conclusion that students need to learn to "reflect" often throughout the year. . . . Teachers need to model what reflection looks like, sounds like, and then talk through thoughts to provide an example to students about how one reflects. . . . We realized students need strategies and procedures to help them open the door to their inner world of learning.

The classrooms of co-curricular teachers tend to be large spaces that can accommodate many people. Additional support personnel in the school, such as library assistants, cooks, or custodians, often want to be involved in student-led conferences. Many schools utilize areas such as the library or gymnasium to provide child care to siblings during student-led conferences. One principal noted, "We provide the library and computer lab, staffed with teaching assistants, for the siblings of those involved in student-led conferences. The informal atmosphere is so inviting!" Kitchen staff plan and prepare refreshments for conferences, often with the help of students. And, all support personnel in the school become excellent "parents" as students rehearse or role-play in preparation for student-led conferences.

With student-led conferences, students, parents, administrators, teachers, and support personnel all assume different roles. Students become leaders. Parents become questioners and active listeners. Teachers, administrators, and others become facilitators and supporters. During student-led conferences, these roles are very clear and are all focused on student learning. In fact, one of the most positive effects of student-led conferences we have seen is that everyone involved experiences increased pride and a re-dedication to promoting and reporting student learning throughout the school building.

CHAPTER 3

Designing Formats for Student-Led Conferences

A s we explained in the Preface, a student-led conference is a conference with parents led by the student. There are many ways to organize student-led conferences, and teachers vary in their format preferences. Important factors to consider when designing a specific format include the age and number of students involved, the flexibility of any previously established school district schedule for conference times, the amount of time available for preparation, the comfort level of all participants with the concept of student-led conferences, and the specific goals for student learning. In this chapter, we discuss several variations in format for implementation in different settings and time schedules (Table 3.1).

Individual or Student-Involved Conferences

Some teachers prefer to conduct what we call a student-*involved* conference. With this type of conference, the teacher takes primary responsibility for directing the conversation, while the student is present to add comments or answer questions. The student is responsible for explaining work samples and answering questions regarding classroom participation. However, the real responsibility for the direction of the conference is with the teacher, as in a more traditional parent-teacher conference.

The student-involved conference can be helpful with very young children. It may also better meet the needs of parents who have specific concerns regarding a child's achievement or behavior in class. One elementary teacher we have observed uses student-involved conferences to develop relationships with parents of first graders for what is often a child's first experience with full-day school attendance. Since parents of first graders often have very specific concerns and sometimes anxieties about student performance, this teacher

Table 3.1 Student-Led Conference Formats

Format	Description	Advantages	Shortcomings
1. Individual or Student-Involved Conferences	Teacher meets with parents. Teacher controls conference. Student is present for only a portion of conference.	1. Good format for very young student 2. Allows teacher and parents to privately share concerns about student 3. Helps teacher develop relationship with parent while still involving child	1. Students are not heavily involved in preparing for conferences or in reporting to parents 2. Takes more time to meet with parents and then involve student
2. Simultaneous Student-Led Conferences With Multiple Families	Four or five groups conduct conference in the classroom at one time, usually in one-half-hour time blocks. Students are responsible for leading parents through a discussion of student work organized in a portfolio. Teacher visits with each family group for a short time.	1. Students take major responsibility for preparation and for conducting conference 2. Students see direct relationship between quality of daily work and report to parents 3. Efficient use of time; teacher can see four families in one-half hour 4. Format is easily adapted for unique scheduling concerns 5. Parent participation is essential and often increases	1. Teacher is not in total control of what is reported to parents 2. Careful preparation is essential; involves preparing students in addition to normal teacher work 3. More difficult to schedule in traditional, 6- or 7-hour daily schedule common to secondary schools

	Description	Advantages	Disadvantages
3. Presentation or Showcase Conferences	Students lead conference to present collection of work to a group or panel that includes teachers, parents, administrators, and other adults such as business or community leaders. Student is questioned by panel on all facets of student work.	1. Excellent model for providing a culminating experience after a long period of time (semester or year of study) 2. Provides opportunity to showcase student growth over time 3. Reinforcing to students to have adult interest and involvement 4. Promotes quality work on part of students as they prepare for panel conference 5. Can be very effective with special needs students or in arts-oriented or career-technical education settings	1. Somewhat difficult to schedule due to number of people involved and time necessary for all students to complete a conference 2. Format does not lend itself to frequent reporting 3. Panel format may be intimidating to some students
4. Portfolio Night	Families of entire classes gather in the school building at the same time on one night to view student portfolios.	1. Effective way to let parents know what students are working on in school 2. Excellent way to celebrate student successes as a school community 3. Promotes parent involvement and a school-family partnership approach to student learning	1. No opportunity for teachers to conference with all families of individual students 2. May be difficult to schedule depending on space available in school facility

(continued)

Table 3.1 Continued

Format	Description	Advantages	Shortcomings
5. At-Home Student-Led Conference	Teacher visits with student and family in their home so that the student may conduct conference while teacher is present to provide comments.	1. Sometimes used when parents are unable to travel to school to be part of regular student-led conferences 2. Provides excellent adult attention to individual students 3. Promotes parent partnership 4. Increases teacher knowledge of family situations and needs	1. Parents do not have access to public displays of student work 2. Parents not able to see student in daily school environment 3. Time-consuming for teacher
6. Electronic Student-Led Conference	Student prepares a digital portfolio and e-mails to parent. Student and parent and teacher then conduct an on-line conversation regarding student progress toward learning goals.	1. Unique way to integrate technology into the reporting process 2. Convenient; can be conducted anywhere there is access to proper technology 3. Teaches student how to use technology in addition to other academic learning goals 4. Good format for parents who may live apart from their children due to extenuating circumstances	1. Requires good access to all technology needed to create digital portfolio 2. Opportunity for face-to-face communication is limited by available technology 3. Requires students, teachers, and parents to be proficient and comfortable with technology

18

chooses to direct the conferences closely. However, he believes that involving students in the experience is very important. He says,

> I chose to adapt the student-led conference because although I think it is important for students to take responsibility for their work, there are some things I want to cover with parents of first graders. For example, they are typically concerned about reading and math skills, so I have the students read aloud and show their parents how we learn to use manipulatives to solve math problems in class. I ask very open-ended questions that encourage students to talk with their parents about learning. Then, to get private time with parents, I ask the student to move to a classroom computer with headphones to play a computer game. This allows enough time for parents to bring up specific concerns or to ask difficult questions in private. I believe that involving students in reporting progress to parents makes them more responsible and thoughtful about what we do in the classroom each day. I have found that this type of conference helps increase self-esteem in my students. They are excited about learning and love to share their excitement about our classroom with their parents. At the same time, I want to make sure parents have enough private time with me to address any concerns.

Again, it is important to consider the number of students involved, the established schedule for conferences, and learning goals for students when choosing a conference format. Student-involved conferences take more time than student-led conferences because the teacher visits with each family at length. With this type of format, only one family is scheduled per time slot, increasing the amount of time needed to complete conferences for all students. However, given young children or children with special needs, whose families may have added concerns, this conference format encourages student responsibility while allowing parents and teachers some time for private conversation. This format may be a good choice for teachers who are considering student-led conferences but who are reluctant to give up more traditional and private parent-teacher conferences. Student-involved conferences are a good first step to see how students and parents respond to student leadership in conferences.

Simultaneous Conferences With Multiple Families

Many school districts schedule parent-teacher conferences two or more times per year during one or two afternoons or evenings. Elementary teachers typically schedule individual family appointments every 15 to 20 minutes; secondary teachers, who often see up to 150 students per day, make themselves available in a central location such as the gymnasium or cafeteria to see parents on a first-come, first-served basis. Elementary teachers often express frustration at being rushed. Secondary teachers are not able to see the parents of all their students during the time allotted. Given these typical district schedules, we have found that scheduling multiple families at one time for student-led conferences works very well. The model that many teachers have easily and successfully adopted is described by Nancy Little and John Allan (1989) in their article, "Student-Led Parent-Teacher Conferences." They write,

> With this method of conferencing, between four and six families can be seen comfortably during one half-hour time slot. . . . To ensure that each family has a personal and comfortable space to enjoy its time together, the room is arranged with four to six separate areas. . . . The teacher joins each family group and gives encouragement and support to the child who leads the conference. The students proceed through the plan for the interview showing, explaining and demonstrating what they have learned at school. (pp. 213-214)

With multiple families conferencing in the room simultaneously, students assume greater responsibility for leading and directing the conference. Typically, students direct their parents to an assigned conference area, explain the goals and purpose for the conference, and then lead parents through a discussion of student work. Often, learning centers are set up around the perimeter of the classroom so that students can show examples of classroom learning activities. Students are free to walk around the classroom to point out bulletin boards and other displays of student work. With this type of conference, the student shows, directs, explains, and informs parents. The teacher acts as a facilitator and encourages student leadership and responsibility. Parents listen actively, ask questions, and comment on student work.

With four families conferencing at one time in one-half-hour blocks, elementary teachers with a typical class load of 25 are able to see all families in a given class within a 3½-hour period. Secondary teachers are able to see many more families than they can through the first-come, first-served model of conferencing. Given two evenings 3½ hours long with five families conferencing at one time in 20-minute blocks, secondary teachers can conduct 105 conferences. Typically, secondary teachers operating in a first-come, first-served model may see 40 to 50 parents. (Specific suggestions on scheduling are discussed in Chapter 6.)

Multiple student-led conferences conducted simultaneously have been successfully implemented at all grade levels, kindergarten through 12, and in a variety of school settings, urban and rural, large and small. This format can be adapted to a variety of elementary and secondary time schedules to create the flexibility for teachers to conference with all families as needed. It is also

easily understood by parents and teachers who are trying student-led conferences for the first time.

Presentation or Showcase Conferences

Another variation on the student-led conference is a presentation or showcase conference. In this model, students lead the conference and present their
work to a group or panel that includes teachers, parents, building administrators, and other significant adults, such as business or community members.
The teacher is one member of the group or panel and asks questions or makes
comments on student work. Parents and other members of the audience listen and ask questions and comment on the work presented.

This type of conference is usually used as a special culminating experience, at the end of a school year or semester, rather than as part of regularly
scheduled district parent-teacher conferences. This is a student-led conference in the sense that the student takes the leadership role in presenting information to parents, and the teacher facilitates the presentation. However,
this type of conference is more involved and time-consuming than the student-led conference formats described earlier in this chapter.

The group or panel presentation is best used when the purpose of the conference is to demonstrate student mastery of specific curricular objectives
and to demonstrate growth over time in knowledge of specific subject areas.
Darling-Hammond and Falk (1997) discuss the importance of using curriculum standards and accompanying assessments to increase student learning.
They advocate the development of benchmarks for student performance at
the end of elementary, middle, and high school. They go on to say that "students' progress toward reaching the benchmarks should be evaluated contin-
uously with in-classroom assessments, including documentation and student work samples" (p. 198). Certainly, a group or panel conference provides
one good way for parents and educators to document and evaluate student
learning progress over time. This type of conference can be very effective in
special education where students demonstrate their progress toward Individual Educational Plan (IEP) goals. Student-led presentations also lend themselves very well to arts-oriented or career and technical education settings.

One positive outcome of a student-led group presentation is that students
tend to take more responsibility for producing quality work on a daily basis.
For a group presentation to be successful, teachers must notify students early
in the instructional process they will be expected to demonstrate their learning through a public presentation. As students become acutely aware of the
fact that they will be presenting and justifying their work to a panel of knowl-
edgeable adults, they tend to take each step of the learning process more seriously. One drawback of this type of conference is that more time and more

participants are required to conduct the conference. Scheduling becomes more difficult.

Group or panel presentations led by students certainly have a place and can be extremely effective in getting students to take more responsibility. However, these cannot be as easily scheduled or as frequently used to report progress to parents as multiple conferences conducted simultaneously.

Other Formats for Student-Led Conferences

Portfolio Night

Some schools plan special events to enable parents to view and celebrate student work. For example, many schools have instituted an event called "Portfolio Night" that is an opportunity for students to present their portfolios to their own parents. Typically, teachers schedule only a portion of their classes to attend a portfolio night because physical space is limited. Students and their parents spread out in designated spaces around the school so that students can share their work. Elizabeth Hebert (1998) describes Portfolio Evening at her school:

> By far, the most powerful celebration of student competence has been the Portfolio Evening. . . . At one of our regularly scheduled conferences with parents, the children are given the responsibility to present their portfolio individually to their parents and to explain to them the process by which the materials were generated, the self-reflections involved in the selection of the materials, the conversations with the teacher that spurred particular choices, and any other aspect of their "learning stories" they want to share. . . . The dates of the Portfolio Evenings appear on the annual school calendar, and parents are also invited by letter. The event takes place over two nights, with half of the class attending each night for approximately 90 minutes. (p. 585)

Other schools have organized portfolio nights in addition to regularly scheduled parent conferences. Teachers give an introduction about the concept to parents at the school's open house event at the beginning of the school year. Teachers then send regular letters home describing what students are doing with portfolios in class and reminding parents about the dates for portfolio nights. The culminating portfolio night is then combined with a pizza party or ice cream social to further encourage parent participation. Portfolio night is a way to report student learning, a time for students to lead meaningful conferences with their parents about student work, and an opportunity to celebrate student learning for all involved.

Portfolio nights are best used in addition to regular parent-teacher conferences because this format does not allow enough time for teachers to meet with each family. As Hebert (1998) notes, the portfolio night is an excellent way to celebrate student competence.

At-Home Student-Led Conferences

Another format for students leading conferences was developed out of necessity by teachers who met with unique challenges in getting parents to come to school to view student work. This format is the "at-home" student-led conference. Students follow the same format their classmates use in leading a conference at school. The difference is the conference is conducted in the student's home. This conference is best used only when parents are physically unable to get to school or when parents are suddenly unable to attend the regularly scheduled school conferences.

Teachers who have used this method report it is very effective in that students are still responsible for leading the discussion of student work. The teacher may or may not attend, depending on family circumstances and preferences. However, the teacher can comment by way of telephone or letter.

The disadvantage of an at-home conference is that parents are not able to see their children in their daily school environment and do not have access to student displays of work. In addition, many parents have speculated that part of the reason their children seem to take student-led conferences so seriously is the business-like environment the school provides. One parent of a second grader reported that the "Friday folder" of student work sent home for the previous week was often ignored. When asked what he learned in school, her son typically responded, "Nothing." After a student-led conference, she wrote, "[I liked] how important my child viewed this experience. . . . My child spent a lot of time telling us about his best papers. This was sort of like a 'formal' Friday folder appointment. He was sure to let us know it was 'student-led' not 'parent-led.'" Many parents and teachers have commented that the "formal" atmosphere of a school conference brings out very positive student self-reflection.

Future Conference Formats

Finally, we can see in the future a new format developing for student-led conferences: the electronic student-led conference. We know that as schools develop greater access to technology for both students and parents, the use of electronic means for reporting to parents has great potential. In an article titled "Digital Portfolios," Wiedmer (1998) points out that the enhanced medium of a digital portfolio offers additional ways to display unique individual talents and abilities. He says,

> Complete with sound and text, digital portfolios display an individual's growth over time through diagrams and drawings or other snapshots of processes and products. They also include digital video/audio testimonies or explanations by the portfolio developer or other persons. Moreover, electronic portfolios can make use of such effects as animation, voice-over explanations of areas of performance, and scanned images that show completed projects or products. (p. 587)

Use of a digital portfolio would also allow parents to view video footage of student performances in classes such as physical education, music, or band, and technical classes such as welding or drafting that are more difficult to capture in a traditional paper-based portfolio. Given access to the Internet, students could potentially send their electronic portfolios to parents by e-mail attachment and then conduct an on-line discussion of student work.

Format is one element that must be well thought out when implementing student-led conferences in a classroom or school for the first time. As noted earlier, scheduling concerns, age and number of students, teacher experience and comfort with the idea, and specific student learning goals for the conference are all factors to consider in designing a successful system for student-led conferences. We have observed that simultaneous student-led conferences with multiple families is one format that can be widely used with all ages, is easily adapted to different school schedules, and can satisfy a wide variety of student learning goals. Teachers who have implemented this format consistently report success and a high level of comfort in their first attempts at implementation. Parents and students we have interviewed and surveyed are consistently positive and enthusiastic about their experiences, and administrators consistently report increased parent participation rates for conferences. Because we have directly observed great success with this format in many different and unique school districts and buildings, this is the format that we have chosen to describe in detail in the remaining chapters of this book.

CHAPTER **4**

Preparing Students to Lead Conferences

In describing how best to prepare students to lead their conferences, a middle school English teacher reports,

> Thinking back to the first time I wanted to hold student-led conferences, I remember my students being petrified when I tried to explain to them what they were going to do. The best preparation was to take each part of the conference and spend time with it. Role playing eases students' minds. I tell them exactly what will happen and let them know that I am in the room to help ease the nervousness. I also tell them the reasons for student-led conferences.

Little and Allan (1989) suggest that teachers who want to implement student-led conferences consider three main phases: (a) preparation; (b) implementation; and (c) evaluation. They also point out that three main groups need to be well prepared for student-led conferences to be successful: students, parents, and teachers. This chapter includes helpful tips and samples of some forms and organizers teachers have used to help students prepare to lead conferences.

Portfolios or Collections of Student Work

The first step in preparing for student-led conferences is helping students create a collection of student work or a portfolio. Johnson and Johnson (1996) define a portfolio as an organized collection of evidence that shows a student's academic progress, special achievements, skills, and attitudes over *time*. Arter and Spandel (1992) expand this definition by saying the collection must include "student participation in selection of portfolio content; the guidelines for selection; the criteria for judging merit; and evidence of student self-reflection." In an article titled, "What Makes a Portfolio a Portfolio?", authors Paulson, Paulson, and Meyer (1991) outline the following eight guidelines for establishing purposeful collections of student work:

1. Developing a portfolio offers the student an opportunity to learn about learning.

2. The portfolio is something that is done *by* the student, not *to* the student.

3. The portfolio is separate and different from the student's cumulative folder.

4. The portfolio must convey explicitly or implicitly the student's activities.

5. The portfolio may serve a different purpose during the year from the purpose it serves at the end.

6. A portfolio may have multiple purposes, but these must not conflict.

7. The portfolio should contain information that illustrates growth.

8. Finally, many of the skills and techniques that are involved in producing effective portfolios do not happen by themselves. (pp. 61-62)

Using these definitions and guidelines, teachers have great flexibility in designing a portfolio system that works in a particular classroom context. Portfolios may span a semester, a school year, or longer. They may be very focused on one subject area such as writing, or they may include work samples from all subject areas. They may represent student achievement in an integrated curriculum or thematic unit of study. Portfolios may be student-directed or teacher-directed or a combination of both. Students may own and keep their portfolios, or portfolios may be passed from teacher to teacher, grade to grade. Student reflection on the work in a portfolio may be written or reflection may occur through dialogue between teacher and student, parent and student, or among groups of students. A portfolio may be a collection of "best work" or it may represent the entire learning process by including samples of errors with student reflection on those errors. It may be contained in a file folder, a pizza box, or on a computer disk.

Whatever form the portfolio takes, it becomes the basis for conversation and reflection in a student-led conference. That is why it is essential to make decisions regarding the purpose and use of the portfolio before implementing student-led conferences. It is also important to schedule time regularly for students to collect and select work and then to reflect upon the quality of work in preparation for the conference.

The Importance of Clear Teaching and Learning Objectives

Teachers who have used student-led conferences for several years report that their most successful conferences happened as a result of setting clear learning objectives for students. Stiggins (1992) describes this as helping students "see the target and then holding the target still." When students understand the learning goals, when the "target" is clear, they are better able to reflect upon and discuss their progress.

Clear learning objectives help students and teachers create meaningful portfolios. Without clear objectives, the portfolio is simply a folder full of work. Both students and teachers sometimes have difficulty deciding what work is important and representative of real growth and learning. Kallick (1993) says that a good portfolio is "initially a *collection* which over time is reduced to a *selection,* which then becomes a *reflection* of the learner." In order for the *collection* to be meaningful, clear learning objectives must be defined. The *selection* process then becomes easier. Students select work samples that show their progress toward meeting specified learning goals. At the elementary level, teachers typically select one learning objective for each subject area and ask students to collect, select, and reflect on work samples from each subject area. At the secondary level, teachers may select one or two learning objectives for each course. The portfolio collection at this level may be kept separate for each course and housed by individual teachers, or work samples from each course may be collated and organized into one larger collection that is managed by a homeroom, seminar, or advisory teacher.

The portfolio collection may include samples of best work but should also include samples that illustrate the process—including errors or struggles—students go through in learning new material or ideas. For example, one of the specified learning goals for mathematics might be, "Given a written description of a problem, students will choose an appropriate strategy for solving the problem and calculate the answer correctly." Students would then be asked to choose samples of daily mathematics work to add to their portfolios to illustrate progress toward this goal. They might select items such as drawings they made to illustrate problems graphically, samples of written calculations, or written tests or quizzes where they had to solve word problems correctly and explain their work. If students are working in groups to meet this same objective, they might include written progress logs where they have recorded information about group cooperation and participation in solving problems together. Students may include teacher comment sheets, their own written reflections of learning progress from a math journal, or samples of worksheets where they made errors and then corrections, including written explanation of why corrections were needed. This is just one example of how a good portfolio collection with clearly identified learning objectives can illustrate student growth over time. A thoughtful and intentional portfolio collection gives parents, students, and teachers a thorough and clear report of student progress.

Much more could be written here about portfolio preparation. We encourage teachers to investigate some of the helpful books and articles on the topic that are currently available. Several are referenced in Resource A.

Portfolio and Conference Organizers

Having established the importance of a student portfolio with clearly outlined learning objectives, we now turn our discussion to samples of some helpful forms and portfolio organizers developed by teachers for use in student-led conferences.

Figure 4.1 is a sample "Conference Organizer" prepared by two fourth-grade teachers. The blank lines on the form for "math objective" or "science objective" were added to highlight specific subject area learning objectives for the time period covered by the portfolio. Using this form, the teacher determines and communicates the learning objective; students find and list work samples representative of their progress toward the objective. This type of form helps students organize a very purposeful portfolio that indicates progress toward classroom objectives. It also promotes student self-reflection.

Another type of organizer designed for upper elementary grades is shown in Figure 4.2. It lists specific work samples that must be represented somewhere in each student's portfolio. It includes a box called "Other Ideas" to encourage students to choose additional favorite samples from any subject area. Figure 4.3 lists possible products or artifacts that may be included in any portfolio collection. Although not exhaustive, it was designed to help students and teachers think about what evidence already exists to illustrate student growth. This list is also a helpful monitoring tool for teachers who strive to include a variety of alternative assessments in their classrooms.

The "Student-Led Conference Organizer" (Figure 4.4) was designed to give students a one-page overview or "big picture" of what a student-led conference involves. There are lists of things to do *before* the conference, things to do *at* the conference, a checklist of what needs to be included in the portfolio, and sections for student and parent comments. This organizer is best used when first introducing student-led conferences to students. Most teachers then prefer to prepare separate checklists for portfolio contents and step-by-step conference procedures.

Figures 4.5, 4.6, and 4.7 are examples of forms teachers have designed at different grade levels to help students stay organized throughout the student-led conference. Students use the form as a checklist as they proceed through the steps of a student-led conference.

(text continues on page 36)

Conference Organizer

Date:

Dear_____ ,

While you look at my work with me, I want you to notice these things about it:

Math Goal: _____

Work Samples:
1. _____
2. _____
3. _____

Science Goal: _____

Work Samples:
1. _____
2. _____
3. _____

Reading Goal: _____

Work Samples:
1. _____
2. _____
3. _____

Writing Goal: _____

Work Samples:
1. _____
2. _____
3. _____

Social Studies Goal: _____

Work Samples:
1. _____
2. _____
3. _____

Other Goal: _____

Work Samples:
1. _____
2. _____
3. _____

These are the things I think I do well: _____

These are the things my teacher thinks I do well: _____

What do you think I do well? _____

Figure 4.1. Conference Organizer

SOURCE: Adapted from work © 1995 Charlevoix-Emmet Intermediate School District

Bailey, J. M., & Guskey, T. R., *Implementing Student-Led Conferences.* Copyright © 2001, Corwin Press, Inc.

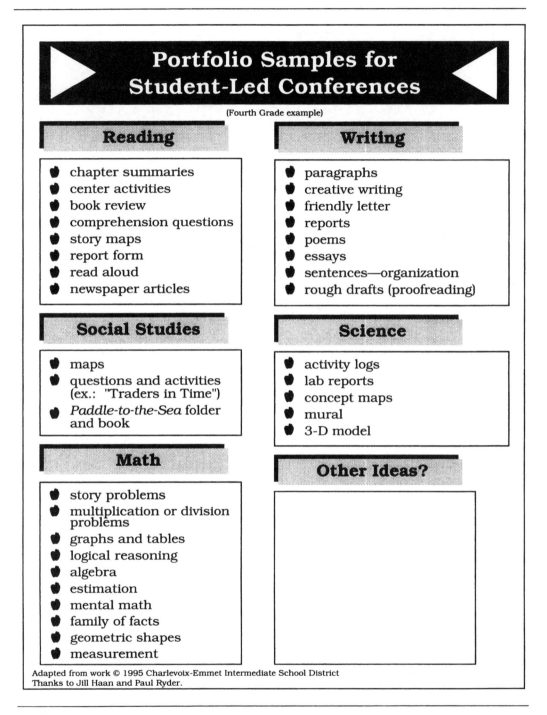

Portfolio Samples for Student-Led Conferences

(Fourth Grade example)

Reading

- chapter summaries
- center activities
- book review
- comprehension questions
- story maps
- report form
- read aloud
- newspaper articles

Writing

- paragraphs
- creative writing
- friendly letter
- reports
- poems
- essays
- sentences—organization
- rough drafts (proofreading)

Social Studies

- maps
- questions and activities (ex.: "Traders in Time")
- *Paddle-to-the-Sea* folder and book

Science

- activity logs
- lab reports
- concept maps
- mural
- 3-D model

Math

- story problems
- multiplication or division problems
- graphs and tables
- logical reasoning
- algebra
- estimation
- mental math
- family of facts
- geometric shapes
- measurement

Other Ideas?

Adapted from work © 1995 Charlevoix-Emmet Intermediate School District
Thanks to Jill Haan and Paul Ryder.

Figure 4.2. Portfolio Samples for Student-Led Conferences

SOURCE: Adapted from work © 1995 Charlevoix-Emmet Intermediate School District

Bailey, J. M., & Guskey, T. R., *Implementing Student-Led Conferences.* Copyright © 2001, Corwin Press, Inc.

Student Products

Advertisement	Filmstrip	Political Cartoon
Animated Movie	Flip Book	Pop-Up Book
Bibliography	Game	Postage Stamp
Art Gallery	Graph	Press Conference
Audio Tape	Illustrated Story	Project Cube
Block Picture Story	Interview	Prototype
Bulletin Board	Journal	Puppet
Bumper Sticker	Large Scale Drawing	Puppet Show
Chart	Letter	Puzzle
Choral Reading	Lesson	Radio Program
Clay Sculpture	Map with Legend	Rebus Story
Collage	Maze	Recipe
Collection	Mobile	Riddle
Comic Strip	Model	Role Play
Computer Program	Mosaic	Science Fiction Piece
Costume	Mural	Sculpture
Crossword Puzzle	Museum Exhibit	Skit
Database	Musical Composition	Slide Show
Debate	Needlework	Slogan
Demonstration	Newspaper Story	Song
Detailed Illustration	Oral Defense	Story Board
Diagram	Oral Report	Survey
Diorama	Painting	Television Program
Diary	Pamphlet	Timeline
Display	Pantomime	Transparency
Edibles	Paper Maché	Travel Brochure
Editorial Essay	Petition	Venn Diagram
Etching	Photo Essay	Web Page
Experiment	Pictures	Working Hypothesis
Fact Tile	Picture Story	Writing Samples
Fairy Tale	Play	Videotape
Family Tree	Poetry	

Figure 4.3. Student Products

Bailey, J. M., & Guskey, T. R., *Implementing Student-Led Conferences.* Copyright © 2001, Corwin Press, Inc.

Student-Led Conference Organizer

Procedures/Things To Do Before Conference:	Portfolio Checklist
1. Make invitation with time and date of conference. 2. Organize portfolio. 3. Practice introductions. 4. Role-play to practice for conference. 5. Set up room.	**Portfolio Subjects to Review:** ❑ Reading ❑ Art ❑ Writing ❑ Music ❑ Math ❑ Science ❑ Social Studies ❑ Physical Education ❑ Group Work ❑ Problem Solving ❑ Special Projects ❑ Behavioral Checklist ❑ Other
Procedures/Things To Do At Conference: 1. Find portfolio. 2. Go to designated spot. 3. Review all parts of portfolio with parents. 4. When teacher arrives, introduce teacher to parents. 5. Ask parents to write a comment. 6. Ask parents to sign guest book. (Do they want another appointment with the teacher?) 7. Return portfolio. 8. Remind parents to fill out evaluation.	These are the things I think I do well: Would you please write a comment after you have seen my work? Student Signature: Parent Signature: Date:

Figure 4.4. Student-Led Conference Organizer

SOURCE: Adapted from work © 1995 Charlevoix-Emmet Intermediate School District

Bailey, J. M., & Guskey, T. R., *Implementing Student-Led Conferences.* Copyright © 2001, Corwin Press, Inc.

Sample Conference Plan

I will do these activities for my family:

☐   Read a book.

☐   Share my poetry journal and read at least one poem.

☐   Share my First Grade Log/Writing Journal.

☐   Share my writing portfolio and read some of my stories.

☐   Share the other work in my portfolio.

☐   Talk about how my work is quality work.

☐   Visit the math center and do a problem together.

☐   Share my handwriting work.

☐   Share and read my Friendship Book.

My Name:_____

Figure 4.5. Sample Conference Plan

Student-Led Conference Checklist

☐ 1. Make sure your teachers know that you are here.

☐ 2. Show your parents where to sit. Get out your portfolio.

☐ 3. Read your welcome letter.

☐ 4. Share your picture and paragraph.

☐ 5. Tell your parents how and why you are a "quality producer."

☐ 6. Begin sharing your work.

☐ 7. Read and discuss your self-assessments for group work and citizenship.

☐ 8. Show and explain what you do best in school (academically).

☐ 9. Write either a short-term or long-term goal with your parents. Include strategies or ways to improve.

☐ 10. Give your parents the homework.

☐ 11. Thank your parents for coming.

☐ 12. Return your portfolio.

Figure 4.6. Student-Led Conference Checklist

Bailey, J. M., & Guskey, T. R., *Implementing Student-Led Conferences.* Copyright © 2001, Corwin Press, Inc.

My Student-Led Conference Organizer

A. Introduction

  1. Introduce parents to teacher.
  2. Find portfolio and lead parents to available area.
  3. Discuss purpose of student-led conferences.

B. Portfolio Organizer

  1. Go over "Linger Over Learning" sheets.
  2. Show examples of quality work.
  3. Explain what makes it quality.
  4. Tell what makes you especially proud.
  5. Discuss what you need to work on and what you can do to improve.
  6. Explain, if needed, why there are no samples of quality work.

C. Behavioral Self Evaluation

  1. List things you do well behaviorally.
  2. Point out areas you need to improve.

D. Goal Setting

  1. Review goals you have set.
  2. Explain how you intend to meet those goals.

E. Parent Input

  1. Show parents questions for which you have prepared answers.
  2. Answer other questions parents have for you.
  3. Encourage parents to ask teacher questions.

F. Teacher Input

  1. Hear teacher's comments to parents and students.

G. Self Evaluations

  1. Hand parents Parent Letter/Conference Evaluation sheet to complete.
  2. Ask them to sign the class book.
  3. Relax and know that you did a GREAT job!

Figure 4.7. My Student-Led Conference Organizer

Bailey, J. M., & Guskey, T. R., *Implementing Student-Led Conferences.* Copyright © 2001, Corwin Press, Inc.

Making Time for Reflection

As we stated earlier, it is important to schedule time regularly for students to collect and select work and to reflect upon quality of work in preparation for the conference. Having students write about their experiences with learning new materials is one way to encourage reflection. Conversations also promote reflection. When students discuss their work with someone else—teacher, parent, or another student—they have to "think about thinking" and then articulate what they have learned. The power of creating a portfolio collection lies in the reflective process and in the writing and conversations about student work (Murphy & Smith, 1990). When students have the time to reflect, they have the opportunity to learn about learning.

Teachers have developed several useful forms to promote student reflection. Figure 4.8, "Lingering Over Learning," was developed by an early childhood teacher but is used widely at all grade levels. It encompasses two different tools to help students reflect. Students may complete a visual map or diagram that shows what they have learned, or they may complete sentence prompts. Many teachers use open-ended sentence stems to engage students in reflection. Figure 4.9 shows a few examples. These are easy to create for different grade levels and purposes. By varying the sentence stems, teachers can provoke students to think in different ways about a piece of work.

Another type of reflection tool is illustrated in Figures 4.10 and 4.11. Students are asked to summarize strengths and areas of concern for parents. Figure 4.12 shows sample "tags" that students complete and attach to portfolio selections. Tags can be designed to target any learning goal a teacher feels is important. Because students like variety, it is important to vary sentence stems or tags to keep students interested and motivated. Using the same format over and over may diminish the quality of student reflection.

Another written tool helps students reflect on their roles and behavior in a cooperative learning base group. Some teachers use cooperative base groups extensively to develop a family atmosphere and spirit of cooperation. One team of teachers with whom we have worked has students assess their work in the group using the tool in Figure 4.13. Students comment specifically on what they do well as a group member and set goals for improvement related to group work.

Reflection through the writing process is something that most teachers value and use frequently. Reflection through conversation is also very powerful. Teachers often raise the concern that there is just not enough time to conference regularly with all students. Johnson and Johnson (1996) propose one way to promote quality conversations about student work in an efficient way: the use of cooperative groups to review individual student portfolios. Each student creates a portfolio. Criteria for success are clearly outlined ahead of time by the teacher. The cooperative group members verify that each individual's

(text continues on page 43)

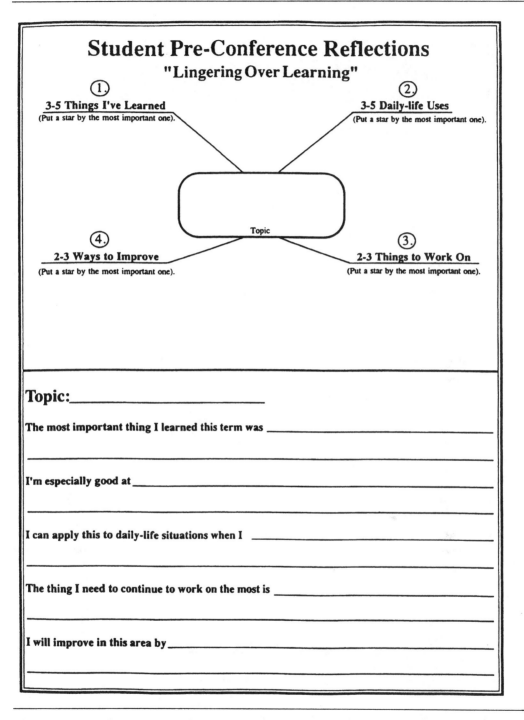

Student Pre-Conference Reflections
"Lingering Over Learning"

① **3-5 Things I've Learned**
(Put a star by the most important one).

② **3-5 Daily-life Uses**
(Put a star by the most important one).

Topic

④ **2-3 Ways to Improve**
(Put a star by the most important one).

③ **2-3 Things to Work On**
(Put a star by the most important one).

Topic:_____

The most important thing I learned this term was _____

_____

I'm especially good at _____

_____

I can apply this to daily-life situations when I _____

_____

The thing I need to continue to work on the most is _____

_____

I will improve in this area by _____

_____

Figure 4.8. Student Pre-Conference Reflections

SOURCE: Copyright 1992 Shelly A. Potter.

Bailey, J. M., & Guskey, T. R., *Implementing Student-Led Conferences.* Copyright © 2001, Corwin Press, Inc.

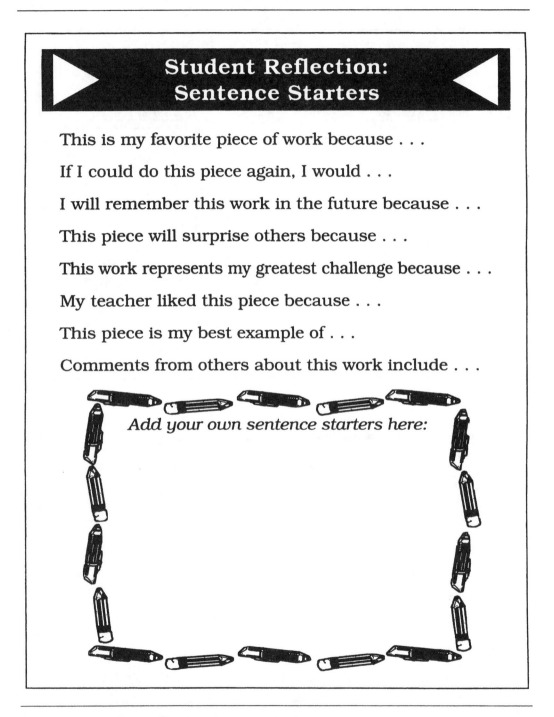

**Student Reflection:
Sentence Starters**

This is my favorite piece of work because . . .

If I could do this piece again, I would . . .

I will remember this work in the future because . . .

This piece will surprise others because . . .

This work represents my greatest challenge because . . .

My teacher liked this piece because . . .

This piece is my best example of . . .

Comments from others about this work include . . .

Add your own sentence starters here:

Figure 4.9. Student Reflection: Sentence Starters

Self-Evaluation Organizer

Dear

As you look over my self-evaluation with me, please notice these things that I feel I do well:

Math: _____

Science:_____

Language Arts: _____

Social Studies:_____

Other:

_____

_____

_____

These are the things that I feel I need to work on:

1. _____

2. _____

3. _____

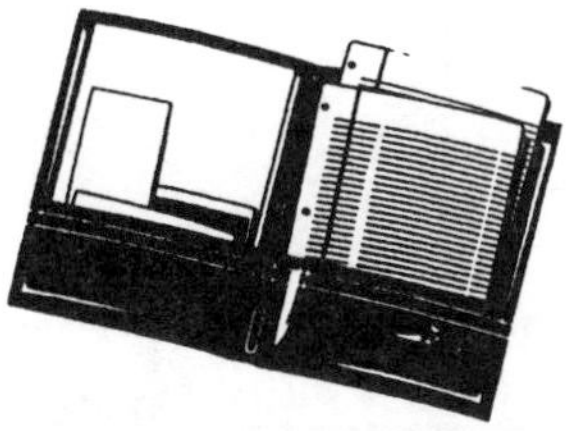

Figure 4.10. Self-Evaluation Organizer

Bailey, J. M., & Guskey, T. R., *Implementing Student-Led Conferences.* Copyright © 2001, Corwin Press, Inc.

▶ My Strengths Are... ◀

Subject Areas	
Work Habits	

▶ My Challenges Are... ◀

Subject Areas	
Work Habits	

Name _____ Date _____

Figure 4.11. My Strengths Are. . .

Bailey, J. M., & Guskey, T. R., *Implementing Student-Led Conferences*. Copyright © 2001, Corwin Press, Inc.

Tags for Student Work

Writing Process:

This piece of work was chosen to show you the steps I use in the writing process. I would like you to notice:

_____

_____

_____

Pride:

I selected this piece of work because I am really proud of: _____

_____

I would like you to notice: _____

_____

Improvement:

I chose this work to show how much I have improved at_____

_____

I used to: _____

Now, I_____

Perseverance:

I included this piece of work because it is something I really tried hard to do well. I want you to see that _____

I am trying hard to_____

I would like you to notice:_____

Figure 4.12. Tags for Student Work

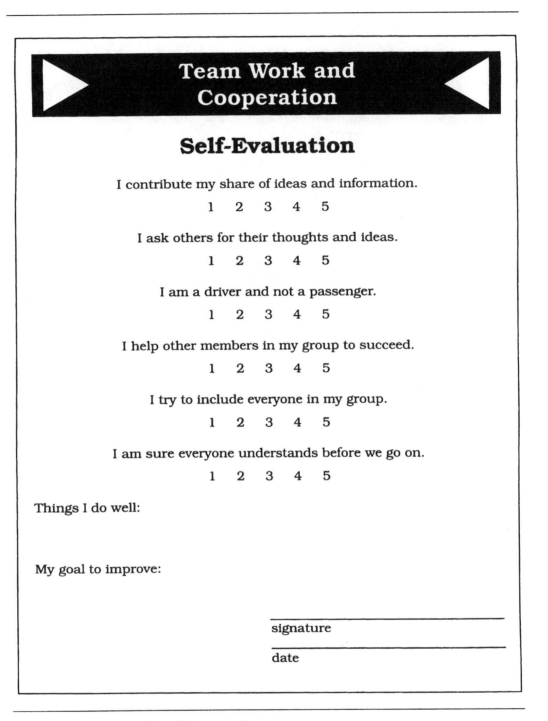

Figure 4.13. Teamwork and Cooperation

Bailey, J. M., & Guskey, T. R., *Implementing Student-Led Conferences.* Copyright © 2001, Corwin Press, Inc.

portfolio meets the set learning criteria. Students receive individual comments and are individually accountable. They also engage in a great deal of group interaction and conversation about each member's work.

Johnson and Johnson (1996) also suggest use of a cooperative group portfolio to "give the support, help, encouragement, and assistance each member needs to make good academic progress and develop cognitively and socially in healthy ways" (p. 7:9). This idea is outlined in Figure 4.14. Through this type of portfolio, students must assess themselves as individuals, and they must assess the group. They are asked to make careful observations of group members' interactions as they work together on projects. This process provides many opportunities for students to reflect on their work from many different perspectives and provides a wonderful opportunity for learning about learning.

Building in time for students to reflect and to learn the language of learning is an important step in preparing students to lead conferences. A high school English teacher summarized the importance of preparing students on a daily basis:

> I give presentations on this topic [student-led conferences], and I am reminded of a time when a teacher asked, "How do I find the time to prepare for these conferences?" My answer probably isn't what he wanted to hear, but I feel very strongly about it. Time shouldn't be an issue. The skills that go into these conferences are skills that should be taught daily in every classroom.

Providing students time for reflection is not only essential to a good student-led conference. It is also essential in helping students make connections to prior knowledge and learn new concepts well.

Tools for Reporting on Behavior or Social Skills

Most teachers and parents place great importance on student behavior and work habits. Since much of life in a classroom involves working with students to develop skills like cooperation, perseverance, teamwork, task completion, punctuality, and the like, teachers want to document and report student progress in these areas to parents. In a student-led conference, this presents a unique challenge. However, teachers who have implemented student-led conferences have created some excellent reporting tools that are both honest and effective.

Cooperative Group Portfolio

What is a cooperative base group?	A **cooperative base group** is a long-term, heterogeneous cooperative learning group with stable membership. It may last for one course, one year, or for several years. Its purposes are to give the support, help, encouragement, and assistance each member needs to make good academic progress and develop cognitively and socially in healthy ways.
What is a group portfolio?	A **group portfolio** is an organized collection of group work samples accumulated over time and individual work samples of each member.
What are its contents?	Cover that creatively reflects group's personality Table of contents Description of the group and its members Introduction to portfolio and rationale for the work samples included. Group work samples (products by the group that any one member could not have produced alone) Observation data of group members interacting as they worked on group projects. Self-assessment of the group by its members. Individual members' work samples that were revised on the basis of group feedback (compositions, presentations, and so forth). Self-assessment of members including their strengths and weaknesses in facilitating group effectiveness and other members' learning. List of future learning and social skills goals for the group and each of its members. Comments and feedback from faculty and other groups

2. The teacher explains individual portfolios. The teacher describes the categories of work samples that students will have to place in their portfolios and the criteria that will be used to assess and evaluate each sample.

3. Group members complete a series of individual assignments related to their learning goals with each other's help and assistance. Compositions, for example, go through a peer editing process to ensure that they meet the criteria set by the teacher.

5. Faculty and group members monitor the groups as they work and collect data on interaction among members.

6. Students select work samples from each specified category to include in their portfolio. Each member explains his or her proposed portfolio to the group. Group members give the student feedback concerning the quality of his or her presentation and help him or her choose the specific pieces that best represent the

7 : 9

Figure 4.14. Cooperative Group Portfolio

SOURCE: © Johnson & Johnson, 1996. *Meaningful and Manageable Assessment Through Cooperative Learning,* Interaction Book Company, 7208 Cornelia Drive, Edina, MN 55435, (651) 831-9500, FAX (651) 831-9332.

Figures 4.15 and 4.16 are examples of elementary behavioral and social skills self-evaluations. Students fill these out and then confer with the teacher, who may add written comments, prior to the student-led conference. The self-evaluation is then added to the portfolio where students take responsibility for sharing it with parents.

The example in Figure 4.17 was developed for middle and high school students. With this tool, students fill out the "self" column using a 4-point rating scale. Then, the teacher completes the "teacher" column, and teacher and student meet to discuss any concerns. The "comments" section is for student or teacher use. Parents see the completed instrument during student-led conferences.

Teachers sometimes raise the concern that student-led conferences do not provide enough private time for parents and teacher to discuss behavioral or social-emotional concerns apart from the student. However, teachers and parents who have used the tools shown above have been extremely satisfied with the accuracy and honesty of student self-assessments during student-led conferences. In fact, several secondary teachers have told us that students with behavior problems tend to write much more critical or harsh assessments of themselves than teachers feel are necessary. Parents report they like the chance to discuss behavior in the quiet, private, and business-like setting provided through student-led conferences. One mother of five children commented that she was grateful for the time she could spend really paying attention to one child. Through this interaction, she was able to discuss things that were difficult to bring up at home in front of siblings.

Good work habits are also important to both teachers and parents. A tool such as the one shown in Figure 4.18 elicits responses from students regarding their progress on learning good work habits like listening, following directions, and using time wisely. Figure 4.19 is a self-assessment of citizenship that also asks students to write their reflections and to set goals for improvement. Finally, a tool called "School Feelings" (Figure 4.20) was developed for second graders to use in student-led conferences. Students include a picture of themselves in their school environment.

The Importance of Role-Playing

To the question, "What is the most important part of preparing students to lead conferences?", teachers who have implemented student-led conferences answer, "Make sure you build in time for role-playing!" Somewhat surprisingly, we get this answer from teachers at all levels, early childhood teachers as well as high school teachers. There is great value in rehearsing with students. A team of elementary teachers told us,

(text continues on page 54)

▶Behavioral Self-Evaluation◀

(Early Elementary)

Student's Name:_____

Date:_____

	My Mark			My Teacher's Mark		
	Most of the Time	Some-times	Needs to Improve	Most of the Time	Some-times	Needs to Improve
Use time well						
Keep hands and feet to self						
Listen						
Follow directions						
Complete work on time						
Put forth best effort						

Figure 4.15. Behavioral Self-Evaluation (Early Elementary)

SOURCE: Adapted from work © 1995 Charlevoix-Emmet Intermediate School District

Bailey, J. M., & Guskey, T. R., *Implementing Student-Led Conferences*. Copyright © 2001, Corwin Press, Inc.

► Social Skills Self-Evaluation ◄

Student's Name:_____

Date:_____

	My Mark			My Teacher's Mark		
	Most of the Time	Some-times	Needs to Improve	Most of the Time	Some-times	Needs to Improve
Cooperates in groups						
Listens						
Shares ideas						
Completes work on time						

Comments:

Figure 4.16. Social Skills Self-Evaluation

SOURCE: Adapted from work © 1995 Charlevoix-Emmet Intermediate School District

Bailey, J. M., & Guskey, T. R., *Implementing Student-Led Conferences*. Copyright © 2001, Corwin Press, Inc.

►Behavioral Self-Evaluation◄

Name: _____

Subject: _____**Teacher:** _____

Please rate yourself in the following areas according to this scale:

4 — Always (100% of the time)
3 — Usually (85% of the time)
2 — Sometimes (Less than 85% of the time)
1 — Rarely (0% to 10% of the time)

Organizational Skills	Self	Teacher
Records assignments in planner		
Records due dates in planner		
Can quickly find assignments, etc.		
Keeps separate sections for each class in notebook		
Keeps notebook cleaned out and up to date		
Cleans locker on a regular basis		
Comments:	**Total:**	

Responsibility	Self	Teacher
Comes to class prepared with all required materials		
Completes the homework on time		
Requests help if needed		
Respects school materials and supplies		
Returns letters, progress reports, etc. in a timely manner		
Comments:	**Total:**	

Work Ethic	Self	Teacher
Uses time in class efficiently		
Does quality work		
Cooperates and works well with others		
Does correctives when necessary		
Offers to help others (voluntarily)		
Seeks extra credit or extensions		
Comments:	**Total:**	

Figure 4.17. Behavioral Self-Evaluation

SOURCE: Adapted from work © 1995 Charlevoix-Emmet Intermediate School District

Bailey, J. M., & Guskey, T. R., *Implementing Student-Led Conferences.* Copyright © 2001, Corwin Press, Inc.

Behavior/Attitude	Self	Teacher
Respects others		
Pays attention in class		
Participates in class on a regular basis		
Does what is requested by the teacher		
Comments:	**Total:**	

Tests/Quizzes	Self	Teacher
Prepares for a test by consistently doing all assignments		
Does correctives as requested		
Retakes test by deadline date		
Shows proof of study		
Comments:	**Total:**	

Lunch/Hallways	Self	Teacher
Follows cafeteria rules		
Follows all school rules		
Respects school property		
Respects the adults in charge		
Passes quietly in the hallway so as not to disturb other classes		
Comments:	**Total:**	

Figure 4.17. Continued

Bailey, J. M., & Guskey, T. R., *Implementing Student-Led Conferences.* Copyright © 2001, Corwin Press, Inc.

▶ Behavior and Work Habits ◀

I feel my biggest **strengths** with behavior are:

_____

_____

I feel my biggest **challenges** with behavior are:

_____

_____

Here's how I feel I'm doing in the following areas:

Listening: _____

_____

Self-control: _____

_____

Following directions: _____

_____

Using time wisely: _____

_____

Working without disturbing others: _____

_____

Respecting others: _____

_____

Working in groups: _____

_____

Figure 4.18. Behavior and Work Habits

Participating in class:_____

_____

I will work on improving:_____

_____

My teacher's comments:

My parents' comments:

Name:_____Date:_____

Figure 4.18. Continued

Self Assessment and Citizenship Self-Evaluation

	1 = needs major work				5 = excellent
Is attentive when others are speaking.	1	2	3	4	5
Shows self-control.	1	2	3	4	5
Respects property of others.	1	2	3	4	5
Respects other people.	1	2	3	4	5
Greets others appropriately.	1	2	3	4	5
Resolves conflicts in a positive way.	1	2	3	4	5
Makes requests respectfully.	1	2	3	4	5
Follows directions.	1	2	3	4	5
Gets teacher's attention appropriately.	1	2	3	4	5
Shows responsibility with given freedom.	1	2	3	4	5

Reflection:

Goal:

Name:_____Date:_____

Figure 4.19. Self Assessment and Citizenship Self-Evaluation

Bailey, J. M., & Guskey, T. R., *Implementing Student-Led Conferences.* Copyright © 2001, Corwin Press, Inc.

► School Feelings ◄

Name:_____Date:_____

I feel best about myself in this class when _____
_____

I have the most fun in this class when_____
_____

I feel proud of myself in this class when_____
_____

I am most relaxed in this class when_____
_____

The best thing I contribute to this class is_____
_____

A picture of me at school:

Figure 4.20. School Feelings

We feel it is very important to talk the language with students long before their conference. The work begins at the beginning of the year as we talk about being self-directed, quality work, reflection, goal setting, portfolios, and more. We feel the children really need to know the vocabulary to live it. During conferences, we watch students use the vocabulary with great understanding. It's fun to watch parents raise their eyebrows when their children use the vocabulary.

Middle and high school teachers, too, report that a key to effective student-led conferences is role-playing so that students begin to articulate the "language of learning." Typically, teachers model a student-led conference for the class. Then, students break into groups and assume the different roles in a conference: parent, student, teacher. Each student has a turn presenting a portfolio to "parents," and the "teacher" walks around the room, encouraging, supporting, and commenting at each group. Many teachers enlist parent volunteers, colleagues, the building principal, or support personnel (e.g., cooks, secretaries, counselors) to play the role of parent. Elementary teachers often link up with a class of high school students who assume the parent role. One elementary principal we know reports that her staff members regularly use high school students for this purpose and that both groups of students thoroughly enjoy the experience. She and colleagues have designed a rating form that older students use to give structured comments to their young charges (Figure 4.21).

To illustrate the importance of role-playing and to address their colleagues' questions about the amount of class time needed to prepare for student-led conferences, two elementary teachers wrote the sample lesson plan shown in Figure 4.22. This outline is easily adapted to different grade levels. We want to note that older students typically do not need a lesson in making proper introductions. However, many middle school teachers tell us that they still review this bit of etiquette briefly with students to stress the business-like nature of student-led conferences.

The more time students have to talk about their work to others, the more they naturally reflect upon their performance and the quality of their work. For this reason, role-playing is an effective way to inspire active learning.

Many teachers have asked us about the time required for preparing for student-led conferences. That is, before teachers implement this idea, they want to know how much additional class time will be needed to adequately prepare students. Teachers who have implemented student-led conferences have found that the time needed to practice introductions and to role-play the conference is approximately three to four one-half-hour sessions at the elementary level and somewhat less for secondary students. It is important to note that other activities, such as preparing written invitations or selecting

(text continues on page 58)

▶ Rehearsal Sheet ◀

Name:_____

Partner:_____

	1st Run		2nd Run	
	Yes	Not Yet	Yes	Not Yet
Looks at Listener				
Speaks Slowly				
Speaks Loudly				
Speaks Clearly				
Good Posture				
Other				

Comments:

Figure 4.21. Rehearsal Sheet

Bailey, J. M., & Guskey, T. R., *Implementing Student-Led Conferences.* Copyright © 2001, Corwin Press, Inc.

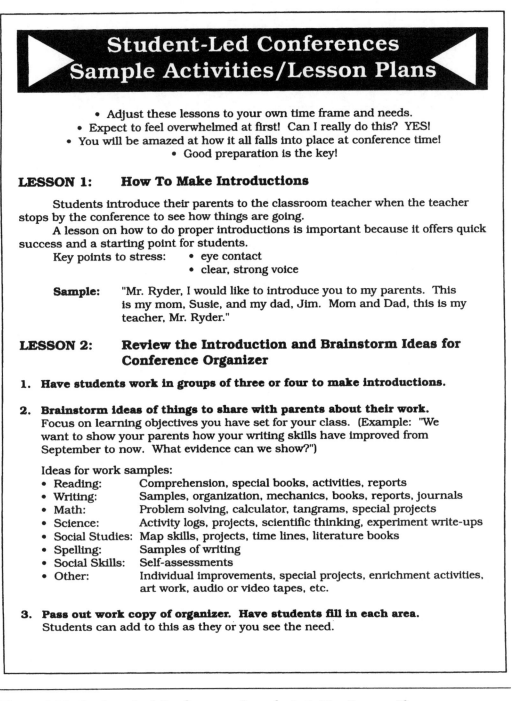

Student-Led Conferences Sample Activities/Lesson Plans

- Adjust these lessons to your own time frame and needs.
- Expect to feel overwhelmed at first! Can I really do this? YES!
- You will be amazed at how it all falls into place at conference time!
- Good preparation is the key!

LESSON 1:   How To Make Introductions

Students introduce their parents to the classroom teacher when the teacher stops by the conference to see how things are going.

A lesson on how to do proper introductions is important because it offers quick success and a starting point for students.

Key points to stress: • eye contact
                       • clear, strong voice

Sample: "Mr. Ryder, I would like to introduce you to my parents. This is my mom, Susie, and my dad, Jim. Mom and Dad, this is my teacher, Mr. Ryder."

LESSON 2:   Review the Introduction and Brainstorm Ideas for Conference Organizer

1. **Have students work in groups of three or four to make introductions.**

2. **Brainstorm ideas of things to share with parents about their work.**
   Focus on learning objectives you have set for your class. (Example: "We want to show your parents how your writing skills have improved from September to now. What evidence can we show?")

   Ideas for work samples:
   - Reading: Comprehension, special books, activities, reports
   - Writing: Samples, organization, mechanics, books, reports, journals
   - Math: Problem solving, calculator, tangrams, special projects
   - Science: Activity logs, projects, scientific thinking, experiment write-ups
   - Social Studies: Map skills, projects, time lines, literature books
   - Spelling: Samples of writing
   - Social Skills: Self-assessments
   - Other: Individual improvements, special projects, enrichment activities, art work, audio or video tapes, etc.

3. **Pass out work copy of organizer. Have students fill in each area.**
   Students can add to this as they or you see the need.

Figure 4.22. Student-Led Conferences: Sample Activities/Lesson Plans

SOURCE: Adapted from work © 1995 Charlevoix-Emmet Intermediate School District

Bailey, J. M., & Guskey, T. R., *Implementing Student-Led Conferences.* Copyright © 2001, Corwin Press, Inc.

LESSON 3:   Teachers Role Play the Conference

Role Play: Two adults are needed to role play the conference with a student. Explain to the students that you are going to model for them what the conference will look like.

Procedure:
- Students enter the classroom and get their portfolios from a designated area.
- They find an open conference table and sit down with their parents.
- When they open the portfolio, the conference organizer will be on top. Students use the organizer to guide them through their discussions of work with their parent(s).
- At some point during the conference, the teacher will come over to see how things are going. Upon arrival of the teacher, the student stops, makes an introduction, and then talks with the teacher briefly about how things are going. Parents may ask questions.
- The teacher leaves the conference to allow the student to continue and to facilitate at other conferences in the room.
- After students have gone through all of the items on their organizer, they return the portfolio to the designated area.
- Any other "wrap-up" procedures should also be discussed with students (i.e. having parents sign a guest book, asking parents to fill out an evaluation of the conference format, etc.).

While it is important to role play how the entire conference will go, you will probably want to break things down into small parts. Modeling how to talk about the work is very important. The most that some students ever tell parents about what they're doing in school is "nothing" so they really don't have an idea of how to talk about their work. Spend time modeling this and give the students time to practice. It is also good to give students some labeling words to use in their discussion, such as, "This is an example of how I use the writing process. Here is my brainstorm sheet, my first draft, etc."

LESSON 4:   Role Playing with Students

- Begin by reviewing the adult role play from the previous lesson.
- Call students up to role play with you. You are the parent.
- Ask students who are watching the role play to comment on strengths and areas that need improvement.
- Discuss how the role play went.
- Allow students to work in groups of four to role play their conference. The students can rotate roles as they practice.

1. Student   2. Parent   3. Parent   4. Teacher/Observer

Figure 4.22. Continued

portfolio samples, are often already part of the regular curriculum. For example, teachers may grade written invitations to parents as a regular assignment that addresses one of the stated classroom writing goals. In addition, the time needed for role-playing or making introductions may fulfill goals related to public speaking or giving effective oral presentations. Thus, the time spent on preparing for student-led conferences may actually provide an effective way to meet other classroom learning goals.

An Opportunity for Students to Set Goals

Many teachers we have observed use student-led conferences as an opportunity to work with students on setting academic or social goals. The student-led conference provides an excellent time for parents to help their children set educational goals and to discuss things that can be done at home to help students achieve their goals. Some elementary teachers use a form like the one shown in Figure 4.23 for this purpose. As part of the student-led conference plan, parents and the child fill out the form together. The form is saved and revisited at a second conference later in the school year. These goal sheets can be saved from year to year. Each spring during student-led conferences, families review the sheet to see what progress has been made. Most teachers feel that instruction and parent involvement in setting and achieving academic and behavioral goals has helped their students achieve at higher levels.

The Importance of Preparing Students

Every teacher we interviewed for this book commented that the preparation phase of student-led conferences is the most important and also the most difficult. With solid preparation, students are confident in reporting their own progress to parents. Teachers are free to listen, comment, encourage, and learn from the experience. And, parents are satisfied that they have a true picture of what their children are learning in school.

We close this chapter on the importance of preparing students with an observation from two elementary teachers who have observed student-led conferences in their classrooms for several years:

When most students come into the classroom with their parents, they really take charge. The ones you worry about daily have a new sense of confidence. The confidence comes from talking about what they know—themselves! It is endearing to watch.

My Goal

Name:_____ Date:_____

☐ Short term or ☐ Long term

GOAL:

_____
_____
_____
_____

Steps I will take to achieve my goal:

1. _____
_____

2. _____
_____

3. _____
_____

4. _____
_____

How my parents and/or teacher/s can help:_____
_____
_____
_____

When will I revisit this goal? What would I like to find?_____
_____
_____
_____

Figure 4.23. My Goal

The preparation phase of student-led conferences includes several steps that we described in this chapter: (a) setting clear learning objectives for students, (b) working with students to create a meaningful and representative portfolio collection, (c) providing time in class for student reflection, (d) creating specific, written organizers and reporting forms, and (e) practicing and role-playing the actual conference. With careful coordination, the activities involved in implementing successful student-led conferences can fulfill existing classroom goals in areas such as writing or making effective oral presentations. Student-led conferences should not be seen as one more requirement to add to an already crowded curriculum. Rather, the activities leading up to student-led conferences can be effective methods for addressing existing curriculum goals, and the conferences themselves provide an effective way to clearly report student achievement and performance to parents.

CHAPTER 5

Preparing Parents and Colleagues for Student-Led Conferences

Preparing students, as discussed in Chapter 4, is just one step in the whole preparation phase of student-led conferences. In this chapter, we offer guidance on how to introduce the concept of student-led conferences to parents and to colleagues within the school system. We share sample letters to parents; ideas for communicating the concept through open houses, newsletters, or other media; and suggestions on how to introduce this innovation to fellow teachers and staff.

The following excerpt from a letter written by parents of a fifth-grade student participating in their first student-led conference illustrates the importance of good preparation:

> First of all, thank you for the time and effort that must have gone into organizing this for the more than forty families participating. . . . What a project!
>
> We arrived with few pre-set expectations about what the conference would look like. It seemed to go just fine. Having a student-led conference every year is a wonderful idea. It reinforces the concept that students are really in charge of their learning. Student-led conferences remind parents that education is a family affair and that children's progress is directly tied to family attitude and support. We applaud your efforts. It would be a definite improvement to the overall school system, elementary, middle and high school, if more teachers and grade levels would follow suit.

This letter is typical of the many parent evaluations of student-led conferences we have reviewed. Parents want to have information about how their children are progressing. Even parents who are reluctant to come to school for other events find student-led conferences both meaningful and satisfying.

Just as students enjoy attention and encouragement for their efforts, parents appreciate regular communication and information about what is happening at school.

However, many parents are accustomed to gathering that information through an individualized parent-teacher conference format that does not involve the student. The idea of students leading a conference may provoke some reluctance on the part of parents. For this approach to work, parents need to understand the reasoning and philosophy behind student-led conferences.

Communicating the Concept to Parents

A meeting is one way to introduce the concept of student-led conferences to parents. Many schools hold an "open house" or "welcome back to school" event at the start of the school year. These provide an ideal opportunity to talk with parents about the conference schedule and change in format. A written summary of what parents need to know could also be distributed during open house.

We know, however, that families are very busy. Attendance is sometimes sparse at school-wide events and there is no time to schedule a special meeting. In this case, a letter sent directly to parents is a good way to communicate that students will be leading conferences. Figures 5.1 and 5.2 are sample letters to parents of elementary students introducing the idea of student-led conferences.

Some schools send regular newsletters to parents. Articles written by teachers or students or by the building principal can give parents further information about the new format and schedule for conferences. Pictures of students preparing their portfolios or role-playing the conference are effective in helping parents understand the process.

Public access television is one other way some schools get information to parents. Students or teachers prepare interviews or informational broadcasts on the topic of student-led conferences so that parents know what to expect. A story in the local newspaper can also be an excellent way to "get the word out."

With the diversity found in most schools today, educators need to use a variety of methods for communicating new ideas to parents. We have found that even with a simple letter, parents are very open and agreeable to the idea of students leading conferences.

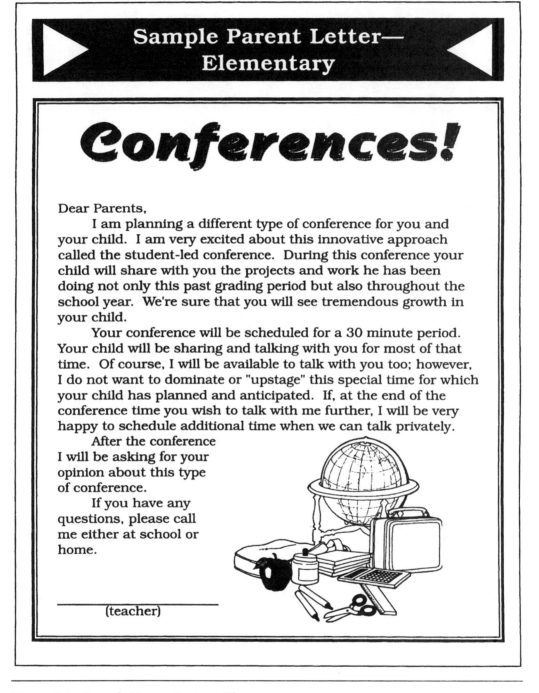

Sample Parent Letter— Elementary

Conferences!

Dear Parents,

I am planning a different type of conference for you and your child. I am very excited about this innovative approach called the student-led conference. During this conference your child will share with you the projects and work he has been doing not only this past grading period but also throughout the school year. We're sure that you will see tremendous growth in your child.

Your conference will be scheduled for a 30 minute period. Your child will be sharing and talking with you for most of that time. Of course, I will be available to talk with you too; however, I do not want to dominate or "upstage" this special time for which your child has planned and anticipated. If, at the end of the conference time you wish to talk with me further, I will be very happy to schedule additional time when we can talk privately.

After the conference I will be asking for your opinion about this type of conference.

If you have any questions, please call me either at school or home.

————————————
(teacher)

Figure 5.1. Sample Parent Letter—Elementary

Bailey, J. M., & Guskey, T. R., *Implementing Student-Led Conferences.* Copyright © 2001, Corwin Press, Inc.

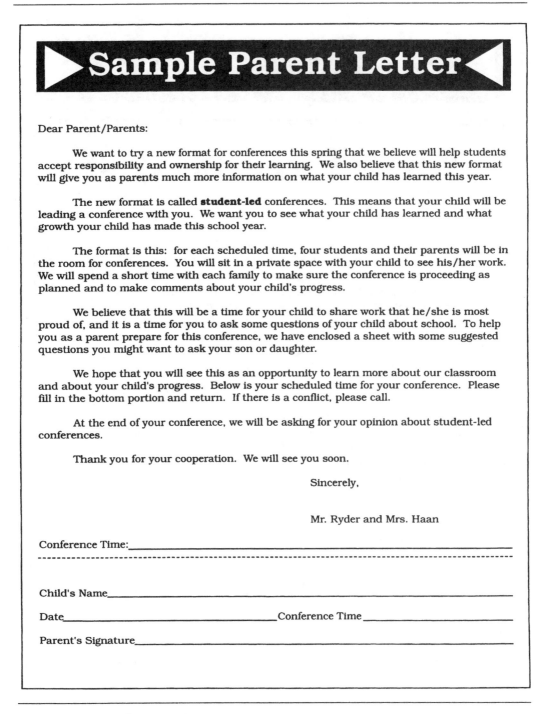

►Sample Parent Letter◄

Dear Parent/Parents:

We want to try a new format for conferences this spring that we believe will help students accept responsibility and ownership for their learning. We also believe that this new format will give you as parents much more information on what your child has learned this year.

The new format is called **student-led** conferences. This means that your child will be leading a conference with you. We want you to see what your child has learned and what growth your child has made this school year.

The format is this: for each scheduled time, four students and their parents will be in the room for conferences. You will sit in a private space with your child to see his/her work. We will spend a short time with each family to make sure the conference is proceeding as planned and to make comments about your child's progress.

We believe that this will be a time for your child to share work that he/she is most proud of, and it is a time for you to ask some questions of your child about school. To help you as a parent prepare for this conference, we have enclosed a sheet with some suggested questions you might want to ask your son or daughter.

We hope that you will see this as an opportunity to learn more about our classroom and about your child's progress. Below is your scheduled time for your conference. Please fill in the bottom portion and return. If there is a conflict, please call.

At the end of your conference, we will be asking for your opinion about student-led conferences.

Thank you for your cooperation. We will see you soon.

Sincerely,

Mr. Ryder and Mrs. Haan

Conference Time:_____

Child's Name_____

Date_____Conference Time _____

Parent's Signature_____

Figure 5.2. Sample Parent Letter

SOURCE: Adapted from work © 1995 Charlevoix-Emmet Intermediate School District

Bailey, J. M., & Guskey, T. R., *Implementing Student-Led Conferences.* Copyright © 2001, Corwin Press, Inc.

Preparing Parents for the Conference

Parents need to know the who, what, when, where, and how of student-led conferences. Once they understand the schedule and place, the format, and the reasons behind student-led conferences, parents sometimes wonder, "What is *my* role exactly?" Providing parents with the list of questions shown in Figure 5.3 prior to the conference helps them understand that their role is to question, to listen, and to gain information. Some teachers tape a similar list of questions to the desk at each conference location to give parents a way to begin conversation when students are nervous. In our experiences, parents appreciate the resource, but often ignore it as the conference unfolds. When students begin to talk about their work, parents are naturally curious, and conversations that may not otherwise take place at home occur very naturally when students lead conferences at school.

Introducing the Concept to Colleagues

As we have worked with new teachers during their first year in the classroom, one of their greatest concerns emerges early in the year: parent-teacher conferences. Inexperienced teachers must evaluate student progress, prepare report cards, and then prepare for face-to-face conferences with parents, often with no outside guidance or coaching. Pre-service teacher training frequently neglects the development of the skills needed to conduct successful conferences (Little & Allan, 1989).

Veteran teachers note different concerns regarding parent-teacher conferences. They express frustration at factors such as low parent participation in past conferences and a lack of responsibility for quality work on the part of students. Veteran teachers sometimes report unpleasant encounters with angry or frustrated parents. They hesitate to spend a great deal of time preparing for conferences that they perceive may become negative or unproductive.

Yet, conferences with parents are an important and expected job responsibility for teachers at any grade level. Because they realize the role that good communication with parents can play in student achievement, many educators are interested in ways to improve the whole experience.

One of the best ways to introduce the idea of students leading conferences is by engaging teachers in a discussion of the advantages and shortcomings of the current system for conducting parent-teacher conferences. Listing advantages and shortcomings helps teachers examine their current practices. Following this discussion, a teacher, administrator, or counselor then presents an outline of the proposed model for facilitating student-led conferences, including the philosophy and rationale behind the idea.

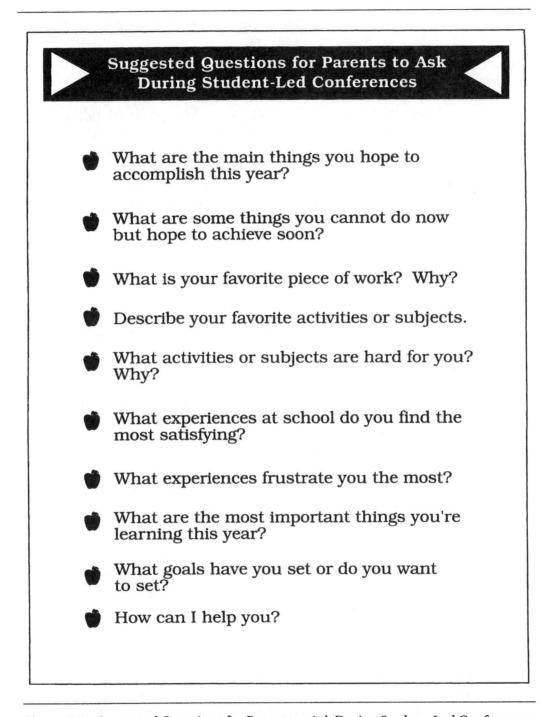

Figure 5.3. Suggested Questions for Parents to Ask During Student-Led Conferences

SOURCE: Adapted from work © 1995 Charlevoix-Emmet Intermediate School District

Bailey, J. M., & Guskey, T. R., *Implementing Student-Led Conferences.* Copyright © 2001, Corwin Press, Inc.

When introducing this new idea to colleagues, it is essential to provide them with the "tools" necessary to make implementation successful. Teachers appreciate sample forms, letters, and possible lesson plans. They typically want to know specifics such as what the new schedule looks like, how best to introduce the concept to students, and what type of support (such as staff development sessions) is available. Teachers also appreciate photographs or video examples[1] of student-led conferences from other classrooms. These help teachers visualize how the concept might translate into the context of their own classrooms.

As this chapter emphasizes, preparation is the key to successful implementation of student-led conferences. Just as students need careful preparation, we must involve parents and colleagues in preparing for this type of conference. Letters to parents, open houses and other school events, media notice through newspapers or public access television, and opportunities for discussion at faculty meetings are all methods for introducing the concept and preparing parents and colleagues for student-led conferences. Given proper and careful preparation, teachers, students, and parents can all relax and enjoy a new type of learning experience.

Note

1. Two available videotapes are referenced in Resource A.

CHAPTER 6

Organizing for
Student-Led Conferences
It's All in the Details

Communication with all participants is key to the success of student-led conferences. In previous chapters we discussed ways to prepare students, parents, and colleagues for this new type of conference experience through forms, letters, classroom discussions, meetings, open houses, and role-plays. Here, we discuss scheduling, room arrangement, and other details that need to be considered when implementing a system of student-led conferences, whether in a single classroom or an entire school building.

A Note About Gaining Acceptance and Faculty Involvement

During training sessions with teachers on the topic of student-led conferences, we are frequently asked, "Must *all* teachers in the school be involved in student-led conferences for this to be a success? Or, can we begin with one or two volunteers?" Our answer is based on knowledge about how successful change happens in classrooms.

As teachers and building administrators, we used to think that to create positive change in classrooms, we first needed to persuade staff members to examine and change their beliefs about teaching and learning. School faculties spent a great deal of time and effort discussing, arguing, and attempting to gain consensus on belief statements such as, "We believe that all children can learn at high levels." The notion was that if teachers examined their beliefs as a group, discussed how to change those beliefs, and wrote a set of statements outlining their new beliefs, then classroom instruction and, ultimately, student achievement, would improve as a direct result of the new belief system. We assumed that the order of change was teachers' attitudes and beliefs first; teachers' practices second; and improvements in student learning last.

Research on educational change has taught us, however, that significant change in teachers' attitudes and beliefs rarely occurs prior to implementation. Rather, it is only when teachers implement a new practice and see success with students that their attitudes and beliefs naturally begin to shift (Guskey, 1986; Huberman & Miles, 1984). Thus, the sequence for meaningful, and enduring, change in classrooms really is change in teaching practices first; improvements in student learning second; and change in teachers' attitudes and beliefs last.

This evidence leads us to recommend that educators "think big, but start small." Teachers who readily volunteer to implement a new practice like student-led conferences are most likely to be successful. By sharing their initial experiences, these successful teachers can help colleagues implement student-led conferences. Experienced teachers become the best resource people for training or organizing student-led conferences in a building.

We always recommend to administrators who are eager to implement student-led conferences that they begin with volunteers. Mandating use of this innovation may lead to resistance, whereas nurturing and supporting volunteers is likely to lead to interest and curiosity on the part of reluctant colleagues. Teachers who feel success often want to share their experiences with colleagues. Parents who respond positively may begin to ask for student-led conferences. And soon, the innovation is practiced by all teachers in a school building.

General Comments on Scheduling

There is no "recipe" or "one right way" to schedule student-led conferences. We have seen many successful but different schedule configurations for student-led conferences. Some factors to consider in setting a schedule are: (a) the length of each conference; (b) the format for student-led conferences; (c) the time already established for parent conferences in the annual district (or building) calendar; (d) the grade level and number of students and teachers involved; and (e) the size and arrangement of facilities. We also discuss some general suggestions unique to elementary and secondary level schedules.

Length

As we conduct training sessions on this topic, teachers at different grade levels express concern over the exact amount of time to allot to each student-led conference. They ask, "Is a half hour too much for a kindergarten student?" or,

"How much time does an eighth grader really need to discuss an English portfolio?" Still others ask, "What if students run out of things to say after 10 minutes?" or, "What if there is way too much material for my students to get through in 20 minutes?" These are legitimate concerns for teachers who are implementing student-led conferences for the first time.

In our experiences, the most effective time allotment for most classrooms and grade levels seems to be one-half hour. Some kindergarten teachers have shortened their student-led conference schedules to 20 minutes, while others have found that one-half hour is very comfortable. We have had teachers at all grade levels describe student-led conferences that have lasted for more than an hour when the schedule allowed (e.g., the last conference slot in an evening or afternoon session). However, we have yet to meet a teacher whose students did not use the entire time allotted. Students and parents seem to have no difficulty "filling the time." On the contrary, teachers' biggest concerns have been keeping the conferences moving on time as families become totally engaged in conversation. Some teachers use a soft bell or chime to signal a "2-minute warning" before the end of conferences. Others also set up a waiting area with chairs and refreshments in the hallway to make for a smooth transition between conference groups.

Format

Given one-half-hour time slots, teachers need to determine format. In Chapter 3, we discussed several different formats for student-led conferences. Here, we confine our discussion to the format most successfully implemented in a wide variety of settings and at different grade levels: simultaneous student-led conferences with multiple families.

Existing Calendar or Previously Established Schedule

Teachers conducting student-led conferences for the first time with multiple families need to examine the amount of time allotted to parent conferences on the existing district (or building) calendar. Many districts allow release time on one or two afternoons for teachers to conduct conferences; others schedule evening conferences. The first step in determining a schedule is to look at the total time allotted to conferences and divide by one-half hour to figure the number of conference "slots" available. Then, determine how many conferences must be scheduled at one time for all families to be accommodated within the existing schedule. Elementary teachers report their greatest success with three to four families in the room per half-hour time slot. Secondary teachers are sometimes comfortable with larger numbers of conferences (up to six at one time) since older students are more self-sufficient. Figures 6.1 and 6.2 show examples of an elementary time schedule and a high school schedule, respectively, for teachers who decided to conduct student-led conferences independent of the rest of the faculty. These classroom schedules were designed to mesh with previously established parent-teacher conference schedules.

As a greater number of teachers choose to implement student-led conferences, district or building schedules can be modified and designed especially to fit the designated student-led conference format.

Elementary Schedules for Student-Led Conferences

Elementary schools typically schedule parent-teacher conferences so that teachers have time for individual conferences with all parents of the 20 to 30 students in each class. Thus, elementary schools have traditionally scheduled longer periods of time for conferences, often 4 to 6 hours of conference time held two to three times per year using a combination of afternoon and evening times. In this case, implementation of student-led conferences is fairly simple. Teachers who schedule four families at one time in one-half-hour time slots can see 28 families in 3½ hours. They actually save time over the traditional conference schedule. Arranging conference times for 20 to 30 students per teacher is very manageable at the elementary level.

We recommend assigning scheduling for student-led conferences to a committee consisting of teachers from different grade levels. This committee can tackle issues such as how best to schedule families who have multiple children attending conferences in a building, how to involve co-curricular teachers meaningfully in student-led conferences, and how to create a schedule that involves minimal conflicts with other district activities.

Scheduling Student-Led Conferences in Middle or High School

Scheduling is often the biggest challenge for educators at the middle and high school levels who want to try student-led conferences. The questions secondary teachers often ask are, "How can I possibly arrange for student-led confer-

Student-Led Conference Schedule—Elementary

Dear Parents:

Please sign up for your first and second choice for a conference time. Remember that your child will be leading the conference. There will be three other families in the room at the same time. I will meet with each family group for a short time to make comments and answer questions. Each family will have an assigned location which is set up to allow for privacy. I would prefer both parents attend the conference, if possible.

If none of these times fit your family schedule, please let me know and I will make another appointment for you and your child to conference. I am also available for a private conference if you feel the need to speak with me further after attending the student-led conference.

As always, please call me with any questions or concerns. Thanks for your support and participation!

_____
(teacher)

Please return the bottom portion of this letter to me at school. Thanks!

Parent Name: _____ **Student Name:** _____

Place a "1" by your first choice for a conference time; place a "2" by your second choice.

Wednesday, November 10th   Thursday, November 11th

_____ 3:30 p.m.   _____ 6:30 p.m.

_____ 4:00 p.m.   _____ 7:00 p.m.

_____ 4:30 p.m.   _____ 7:30 p.m.

_____ 5:00 p.m.

_____ I will need to schedule a conference on another day.

Please call me at _____ (phone). Thank you.

Figure 6.1. Student-Led Conference Schedule—Elementary

Bailey, J. M., & Guskey, T. R., *Implementing Student-Led Conferences.* Copyright © 2001, Corwin Press, Inc.

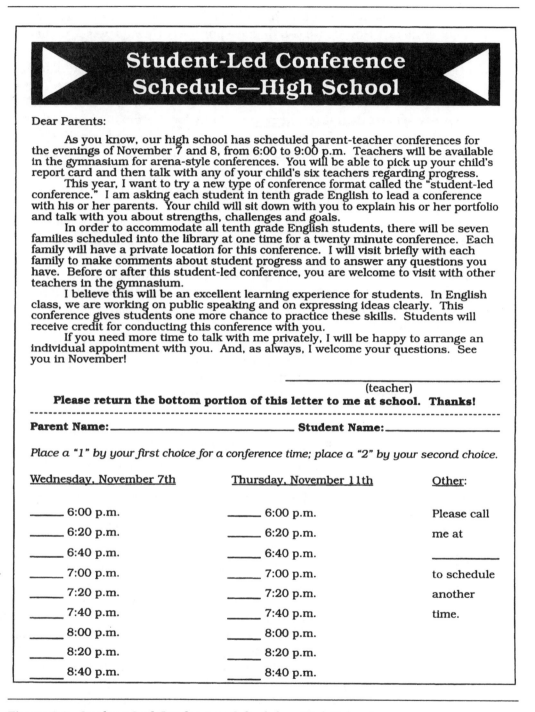

Student-Led Conference Schedule—High School

Dear Parents:

As you know, our high school has scheduled parent-teacher conferences for the evenings of November 7 and 8, from 6:00 to 9:00 p.m. Teachers will be available in the gymnasium for arena-style conferences. You will be able to pick up your child's report card and then talk with any of your child's six teachers regarding progress.

This year, I want to try a new type of conference format called the "student-led conference." I am asking each student in tenth grade English to lead a conference with his or her parents. Your child will sit down with you to explain his or her portfolio and talk with you about strengths, challenges and goals.

In order to accommodate all tenth grade English students, there will be seven families scheduled into the library at one time for a twenty minute conference. Each family will have a private location for this conference. I will visit briefly with each family to make comments about student progress and to answer any questions you have. Before or after this student-led conference, you are welcome to visit with other teachers in the gymnasium.

I believe this will be an excellent learning experience for students. In English class, we are working on public speaking and on expressing ideas clearly. This conference gives students one more chance to practice these skills. Students will receive credit for conducting this conference with you.

If you need more time to talk with me privately, I will be happy to arrange an individual appointment with you. And, as always, I welcome your questions. See you in November!

_____
                                                                        (teacher)
Please return the bottom portion of this letter to me at school. Thanks!

Parent Name:_____ **Student Name:**_____

Place a "1" by your first choice for a conference time; place a "2" by your second choice.

Wednesday, November 7th	Thursday, November 11th	Other:
_____ 6:00 p.m.	_____ 6:00 p.m.	Please call
_____ 6:20 p.m.	_____ 6:20 p.m.	me at
_____ 6:40 p.m.	_____ 6:40 p.m.	_____
_____ 7:00 p.m.	_____ 7:00 p.m.	to schedule
_____ 7:20 p.m.	_____ 7:20 p.m.	another
_____ 7:40 p.m.	_____ 7:40 p.m.	time.
_____ 8:00 p.m.	_____ 8:00 p.m.	
_____ 8:20 p.m.	_____ 8:20 p.m.	
_____ 8:40 p.m.	_____ 8:40 p.m.	

Figure 6.2. Student-Led Conference Schedule—High School

Bailey, J. M., & Guskey, T. R., *Implementing Student-Led Conferences.* Copyright © 2001, Corwin Press, Inc.

ences when I am just one of six (or seven or eight) teachers responsible for the same students? How do we coordinate a portfolio? How do we set a schedule for 125 students and their parents?"

Secondary schools on a block schedule have an advantage here. Often, in a block schedule, time is set aside for an "advisory" or "seminar" or "homeroom" period where one teacher sees 20 to 25 students on a regular basis. The advisory teacher then takes the responsibility for coordinating portfolio collection and selection and for scheduling student-led conferences for only those students. Advisory period time is spent preparing the portfolio, roleplaying conferences, inviting parents, and attending to other details necessary to make conferences a success. During scheduled times, the teacher or advisor facilitates student-led conferences in his or her classroom, taking time to comment and answer questions with each family group. If parents have specific questions regarding a particular subject area, the advisor puts parents in touch with that teacher to make a separate conference appointment. If teachers regularly use the advisory or seminar period to monitor student progress in all subject areas and to help students create a portfolio collection that is truly representative of student achievement, student-led conferences run smoothly and are very effective.

For secondary schools not on a block schedule and with no scheduled advisory time, scheduling presents a bigger challenge but is certainly possible. If all teachers in a building want to implement student-led conferences, a schedule can be specially created to accommodate the required number of students. Students can be scheduled for conferences using classes that are required of all students at a given grade level. For example, if all ninth graders are required to take an English class, the ninth-grade English teachers take responsibility for scheduling and preparation for student-led conferences. Likewise, 10th-grade math teachers, 11th-grade history teachers, or 12th-grade government teachers schedule students into conference slots and coordinate student portfolios.

Given responsibility for scheduling approximately 125 student-led conferences, we recommend that teachers use 20-minute time slots (three conference times per hour). This means that with six students and their parents conducting conferences in a classroom at one time, teachers would need approximately 7 hours of conference time. Figure 6.3 illustrates a sample schedule for one teacher. A scheduling committee composed of faculty members from each grade level and subject area should be created to oversee room assignments, to coordinate conferences for families with multiple students in a building, and to set a schedule of times and dates that best accommodates all grade levels and subject areas.

Some secondary schools that have implemented student-led conferences have started at one grade level or in one subject area or with one team of teachers to try the idea. For example, a humanities teacher and business services teacher we know shared the same group of ninth graders who were

English 9 Room 210	Student 1	Student 2	Student 3	Student 4	Student 5	Student 6
November 7						
6:00-6:20 PM						
6:20-6:40 PM						
6:40-7:00 PM						
7:00-7:20 PM						
7:20-7:40 PM						
7:40-8:00 PM						
8:00-8:20 PM						
8:20-8:40 PM						
8:40-9:00 PM						
November 8						
6:00-6:20 PM						
6:20-6:40 PM						
6:40-7:00 PM						
7:00-7:20 PM						
7:20-7:40 PM						
7:40-8:00 PM						
8:00-8:20 PM						
8:20-8:40 PM						
8:40-9:00 PM						
November 9						
6:00-6:20 PM						
6:20-6:40 PM						
6:40-7:00 PM						

Sample Secondary School Schedule Grid for Student-Led Conferences

Note: All students at a grade level are assigned to a student-led conference through one class that is required at that grade level (i.e. ninth grade English). Teachers work together to ensure that all students have a scheduled conference time. Room assignments are coordinated by a faculty committee to eliminate conflicts.

Figure 6.3. Sample Secondary School Schedule Grid for Student-Led Conferences

NOTE: All students at a grade level are assigned to a student-led conference through one class that is required at that grade level (e.g., ninth-grade English). Teachers work together to ensure that all students have a scheduled conference time. Room assignments are coordinated by a faculty committee to eliminate conflicts.

Bailey, J. M., & Guskey, T. R., *Implementing Student-Led Conferences.* Copyright © 2001, Corwin Press, Inc.

required to take both subjects. The humanities teacher required students to assemble a portfolio of humanities projects throughout the year. The business teacher taught students how to import humanities documents using a scanner or e-mail to create an electronic portfolio. Students then created Power-Point™ presentations to share with parents. The two teachers scheduled student-led conferences, four at one time in one-half-hour time blocks, in the business lab so that students could share their electronic portfolios. Both teachers circulated around the room to make comments and answer questions. Parents we interviewed were delighted at the quality of student work and now look forward to such conferences each year. Given the success these teachers experienced, colleagues in the same high school are now teaming to find ways to implement student-led conferences. One of the high school faculty's goals is to implement student-led conferences building-wide over a 2-year period.

Other questions that secondary school teachers typically ask are, "How can I facilitate conferences for students who are presenting a portfolio containing work from subjects I do not teach?" and "How can I answer questions about someone else's class?" With good preparation and an adequate number of work samples from each class, parents have most questions answered through the student-led conference. Also, teachers from each subject area may offer written comments that are added to students' portfolios. The teacher facilitating student-led conferences may not be able to answer subject-specific questions. However, the facilitator can offer advice to parents on how to find answers and can work with the family group to create a plan to address specific concerns. Parents and students appreciate the time to talk about schoolwork in a business-like atmosphere. Most parents report that time spent viewing and discussing a portfolio of student work provides them with much better and more accurate information than any report card or letter grade.

The final question we often hear from secondary teachers is, "Why should we do this instead of our traditional arena-style conferences? I like to talk with parents individually, and I don't always want the student present to hear what I say!" We urge teachers to carefully examine the total *system* for reporting student progress to parents. Certainly, a student-led conference is one effective way to report to parents. However, no one method can fulfill all reporting requirements. There are times when teachers need to schedule private, individual conferences with parents. At other times, written reports are helpful and necessary.

Constant communication is essential if teachers and parents are to be effective partners in helping students achieve at higher levels. Each school needs to create a system for reporting student progress that fits its unique context and addresses the special needs of parents, teachers, and students in the school community. Though we encourage educators to implement student-led conferences, we urge faculties to discuss and create a larger system for reporting student progress that is consistent and comprehensive.

Arranging Facilities

Teachers at all grade levels emphasize the importance of arranging physical space to create an inviting, comfortable environment. Conference tables or desks must be large enough to accommodate students and their parents comfortably. Spacing between conference sites must be adequate to ensure family privacy while allowing for appropriate noise levels.

The number of conferences being held in a room at one time is an important consideration for facility arrangement. Experienced teachers report that with only two conferences in a classroom at one time, privacy is actually more difficult. One family may overhear another's conversation. Yet, given the size of most classrooms, more than five or six conferences going on at once may create pandemonium when young children are leading conferences. Thus, four families at a time, one placed in each corner, is an effective arrangement for most average-sized classrooms.

Sometimes teachers use soft background music to create a relaxing environment and to create privacy when too few people are in the room. Music also helps calm students who may be nervous when starting the conference.

Bulletin boards displaying student artwork, pictures of students taken "in action" during class, or current academic work samples are excellent tools in helping parents understand what learning goals are stressed in the classroom. Students can spend part of the conference time explaining the work on display.

Students of all ages seem to enjoy decorating the classroom before student-led conferences. Some teachers hang signs above each conference "station" listing family names and times for conferences so that students know exactly where to sit. In some classrooms, students decorate with flowers or some sort of centerpiece on the table or desks used for conferences. Conference stations equipped with pencils, pens, and paper make it easy for parents to take notes during the conference. Often, teachers tape an outline to the desk at each station so that students remember all required conference steps.

Finally, many teachers use a "guest book" or sign-in sheet to record parent participation during student-led conferences. This practice may be continued throughout the school year. Parents or visitors are invited to write comments each time they visit the classroom. Pictures may be added. The guest book then becomes a historical record of events for the class. Teachers tell us they have used such books very creatively in teaching social studies or other subjects where students need to look back over time.

Attending to Amenities: Arranging Child Care and Refreshments

Because parents with several children may find it difficult to attend any type of parent-teacher conference, many schools now arrange for on-site child care as a helpful service. Parents need to be able to concentrate on one child at a time to truly listen and to learn about student achievement. When other siblings are present, interruptions inevitably change the tone of the conference. Many schools notify parents ahead of time about child care service. They arrange to have high school students or other volunteers greet parents at the door and take siblings to a designated room for supervision during the conference. Parents can then concentrate on the child leading the conference.

Refreshments in the classroom or in a central location are one other amenity both parents and students appreciate. Providing simple food and drink sends the message that the school welcomes and appreciates participation in conferences and school activities.

Encouraging Parent Participation

As we outlined earlier, letters to parents, information printed in school newsletters, video spots on public TV, and newspaper articles are all ways to communicate to parents about student-led conferences. Sometimes, however, a personal contact is most effective in encouraging parent participation in conferences. Teachers make telephone calls or seek out parents at public events to stress the importance of attending conferences. One elementary school faculty decided to make personal calls to every home to invite parents to their "first annual" student-led conferences. The result was 100% parent participation school-wide!

Schools we have visited have used pizza parties, ice cream socials, or other family events to encourage parents to come to conferences. Secondary teachers often require that students lead a conference as part of a grade for English or other appropriate subject area. When students are responsible for preparing special invitations to parents and helping with scheduling actual conference times, parent participation increases.

Careful attention to scheduling, room arrangement, child care, refreshments, and other amenities helps make student-led conferences successful. Involving students in the preparation only increases their pride and ownership in the process. And, special efforts to encourage parent attendance further emphasize the importance of communicating about student learning—the major goal of a student-led conference.

CHAPTER 7

Anticipating and Handling Unique Situations

S ometimes, even with careful scheduling, proper parent notification, comfortable facilities, and attention to details such as child care, refreshments, and other amenities, unanticipated and often unique problems can occur. A first-grade teacher described the following experience the first time she tried student-led conferences:

> I thought I had fully prepared students and parents for this new experience. We practiced in class. We decorated the room. I prepared special invitations to parents. The night of conferences, one parent came without her son. When I reminded her this was a conference led by her son and asked where he was, she said, "He's home sleeping. It's 8:00 p.m. and he needs to be in bed so he can get up the next morning."
>
> I learned a valuable lesson. I hadn't anticipated that our evening schedule really didn't fit first graders.

A middle school teacher described the following scenario:

> I scheduled conferences for students in my homeroom and was feeling very proud that all parents had confirmed their attendance. During the first conference of the evening, I had four families in the room. Things were going fine until about 10 minutes into the conferences. Suddenly, chaos erupted. I realized the four students I had scheduled at one time happened to be boys who had all been diagnosed with Attention Deficit Hyperactivity Disorder (ADHD). All four were on Ritalin. And, it seemed to me that none had taken their meds! Needless to say, I learned to be more selective in scheduling.

Situations such as these are difficult to anticipate, especially when implementing an innovation for the first time. We outline here six difficult situations teachers have experienced with student-led conferences. They include: (a) parents who cannot attend conferences; (b) potentially abusive parents; (c) extra guests who arrive for conferences; (d) students with special needs; (e) very young students; and (f) non-English-speaking parents or students. In this chapter, we describe and present suggestions for handling each situation.

Situation 1: Parents Who Cannot Attend Conferences

Inevitably, conflicts will occur with the schedules of some parents. Business travel or special family circumstances may make it impossible for either parent to attend a conference. When conflicts are clear ahead of time, students should be encouraged to invite a grandmother or grandfather, aunt or uncle, close family friend, or special teacher to attend conferences. Students want to feel "part of the action," so the experience of leading a conference with other classmates present is an important one. Any adult who cares for the student can be a fine substitute during a student-led conference.

Sometimes conflicts occur at the last minute and parents are suddenly unable to attend a scheduled conference. In cases such as this, we have found it best to schedule a separate conference at school so that families have a chance to see student work and to talk with the teacher in a business-like setting.

Teachers have also allowed students to conduct conferences at home in special circumstances. In the words of a middle school teacher,

> Every year I do have one or two high achieving students whose parents can't come to conferences. The students are disappointed because they have prepared so well. I let those portfolios go home along with a parent evaluation sheet that is returned to me so I know the conference actually took place. I only allow that for students I *know* will hold the conference. With others, I hold the conference at school with a pseudo parent.

Teachers have also encountered situations where parents are disabled or ill, physically unable to come to school. In this case, teachers have volunteered to visit the home so that students can conduct a conference with the teacher present to provide comments and answer questions. This calls for extra work, but teachers report that the appreciation from parents and the benefits to children make the effort worthwhile.

Situation 2: Potentially Abusive Parents

Some teachers have described concerns or even fears in trying student-led conferences with parents who might be verbally abusive, angry, or explosive. One teacher told us,

> I was extremely worried about Mr. X. I knew that there was physical abuse in the home, and in fact, I had reported my suspicions to authorities. However, I felt it was very important for this student to attend conferences with the rest of the class. He was already "at-risk" and I didn't want to alienate him further from his classmates. I called Mr. X ahead of time and I paid special attention during the conference. My fears were unfounded. Mr. X came to me at the end of the conference, crying, and told me that he was surprised and happy at what his son had achieved. This experience alone probably did more for the student's self-esteem than anything else I did in class all year.

To avoid embarrassment to students or families, we recommend that teachers take several precautions. First, carefully schedule parents who present potential problems in the room with families who are sure to be supportive and understanding. Next, make a personal contact ahead of time to emphasize the importance of the conference, to outline clearly what the experience will be like, and to answer any questions parents may raise about students' leading conferences. Finally, greet parents at the door and give special attention to families who might need extra support in keeping the conference tone positive.

All teachers who expressed an initial fear told us that after careful preparation and communication with parents ahead of time, conferences were very positive.

Situation 3: Extra Guests Who Accompany the Family to Conferences

Several teachers told us the first time they tried student-led conferences, they did not anticipate that parents would arrive with toddlers, older brothers and sisters, aunts or uncles, and even the family dog! One quick-thinking teacher described how he pulled out pattern blocks and other math manipulatives to keep two young toddlers busy in a corner of the room while parents attended conferences.

It is important to communicate to parents through preparatory letters, telephone calls, or meetings that student-led conferences are a time to give individual attention to each child. Invitations should emphasize that the scheduled appointment includes the student and parents. In addition, many schools offer organized child care in the school building so that siblings can be supervised in another room while parents attend conferences. Finally, we recommend that teachers have games, crayons, and drawing paper or other fun activities available in the room for those occasions when siblings do accompany the family to student-led conferences.

Adults—other than parents—who accompany the family to conferences may be invited to participate if space is adequate. Students take great pleasure in showing their work to caring family members or friends who show a special interest. A grandmother or grandfather, aunt or uncle, or special family friend is likely to ask different questions than parents. This can be a very positive way to encourage students to reflect differently on their work and to view achievement from a new perspective.

At times, teachers have scheduled "family conferences" where students explain their work to the entire family or a group of family and close friends. As we explained in previous chapters, teachers need to carefully determine the goals for a student-led conference. If the primary goal is to allow students to showcase their best work, a family conference may be a very positive experience. However, when students are being asked to explain work in detail, report progress to parents, reflect, and set goals, having a large group present can be too overwhelming or confusing for everyone. Teachers must design the system for student-led conferences that will best help students meet designated conference goals.

Situation 4: Students With Special Needs

We often get questions about how special education students perform during student-led conferences. We have observed many students with learning or emotional problems conducting student-led conferences very successfully. In fact, student-led conferences provide a chance for students who routinely experience classroom failure or difficulties to take charge and to talk about what they know best—themselves!

The key to success for students with special needs is careful preparation. Some students require extra practice and role-playing. They need to work on the language and vocabulary necessary to describe what they are doing in class. For example, students may need to explain that they are "subtracting two-digit numbers and regrouping" or that they are "editing work for punctuation errors." Students need to be able to express their learning goals effectively. For students with reading difficulties, it is essential that the conference organizer be written at an appropriate reading level or include picture cues. The example describing Attention Deficit Hyperactivity Disorder (ADHD) students included at the beginning of this chapter points out the importance of engineering a schedule that accommodates special student or family needs. For example, teachers might schedule conferences after a meal for students with hypoglycemia or diabetes, reduce the number of distractions in the room for students with ADHD, or build in extra time for increased teacher support and encouragement for students with emotional impairments or autism.

Teamwork is another key to success for special education or special needs students. Special education personnel and school counselors are excellent resource people who can help prepare students for conferences. They have knowledge and expertise that can be invaluable to the regular classroom teacher, and they can function as an "extra pair of hands" in preparing student portfolios, role-playing, or preparing parents for this new experience.

We have seen students with all types of disabilities and special needs be extremely successful leading their own conferences. The following comments from the parent of an elementary student struggling with emotional issues illustrates the power a student-led conference can have:

> Emily has had difficulty with self-esteem. I expected her to be nervous, uncomfortable, but she was confident and well prepared. During the conference, she identified her strengths, didn't dwell on weaknesses. Conducting the conference seemed to give her confidence and I saw pride and maturity that is so rarely demonstrated by her!
>
> I was extremely impressed with the conference. However, I'm not sure it would have been successful if it had not been a part of your [classroom teacher's] teaching methods and philosophy. I can't begin to tell you how pleased and grateful I am that Emily was fortunate to be placed in your classroom. This year has been a turning point for her.

Situation 5: Very Young Students

Pre-school (4-year-old) and kindergarten children have been very successful with student-led conferences when teachers make some minor adaptations to the system we have outlined for use with older children (multiple families conducting one-half-hour conferences simultaneously).

One adaptation involves scheduling. We recommend that scheduled conference times be shortened to 20 minutes each. This is an adequate amount of time for very young children to share their work with parents. Given longer blocks of time, some students at this age begin to drift off task.

Another adaptation that is necessary is a conference organizer containing picture cues. Kindergarten students are easily able to follow picture cues to complete all conference tasks (see Figure 7.1). With pre-school students, teachers have found it effective to provide a very simple written list of directions to parents. A sample is shown in Figure 7.2. Parents cue children about the tasks that need to be completed during the conference. With a simple prompt from parents, 4-year-old children are very capable of showing their work and explaining centers or other daily classroom routines.

With very young children, many teachers have found that non-traditional portfolio containers work best. For example, teachers use pizza or cereal boxes to hold student work. These work particularly well for oversized pieces of art work. Students enjoy decorating their portfolio containers, and this activity fulfills a learning objective for art.

Specific learning center activities designed for families also work well for student-led conferences with young children. That is, students lead their parents through a series of typical classroom activities such as creating a simple art project, "reading" a book together, writing in a journal, or making a snack to eat during the conference (see Figure 7.3).

One pre-school teacher we interviewed gives parents a set of written directions for the conference that lists specific steps to be completed. Then, she visits with each family group to report student progress. Finally, she encourages families to tour the room and use materials that are available for play. This teacher works in a special program with families of 4-year-olds labeled at-risk for school failure. She told us that prior to implementing student-led conferences, she would typically see the parents of only 4 out of 36 students. Many of these parents had experienced school failure themselves, and she reasoned that coming back into any school setting might be difficult. So, she stopped scheduling separate, formal conferences and began inviting parents to school to have their children share their work in a relaxed, informal atmosphere. To keep things informal, she does not make special appointments with parents. Rather, parents are invited to bring their children to the classroom any time between the hours of 11:00 a.m. and 7:00 p.m. on a designated day (see Figure 7.4). The teacher is available throughout that time in order to accommodate work schedules and the special needs of families in her program. This relaxed, family-oriented system has been extremely successful: The parents of all 36 students now attend student-led conferences.

(text continues on page 89)

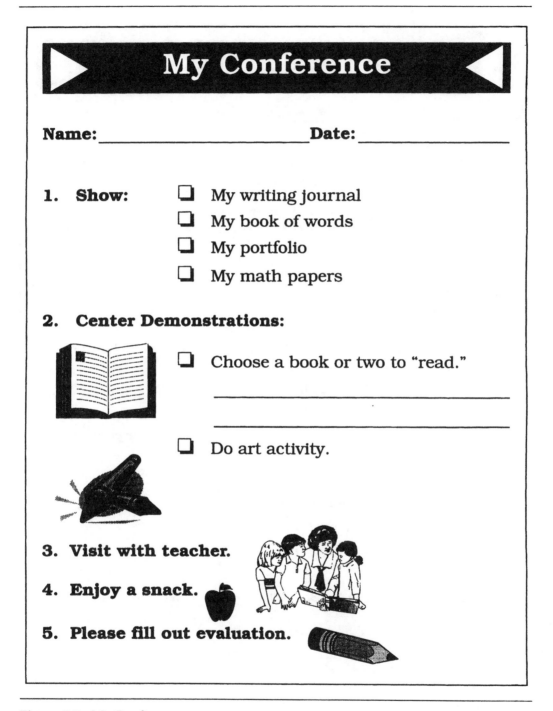

Figure 7.1. My Conference

►Welcome To Conferences◄

(Pre-school Program)

Summary Reports:

Please take time to look over your child's summary report. If you have any questions or concerns, please discuss with me. You will notice that much of the information on the report is similar to the last report because there are certain areas where we consistently document progress. The reports are also given to next year's teacher, so we want them to reflect their overall performance.

Activities:

- Help yourself to a snack!
  Follow the directions for a yummy treat!!!

- Please help your child make a flower for the bulletin board out of the supplies on the table.

- Have your child share his/her journals with you.

- Have your child share his/her books with you.

- Have your child show you his/her work around the classroom.

Other:

- Sign-up for Kindergarten teacher home visit.

- Sign up for volunteer times.

- Make sure that you are not on teacher's list for other information needed before you leave!

It is very important to your child to see you interested in school!

Thanks for coming!!!!!

Figure 7.2. Welcome to Conferences (Pre-School Program)

Bailey, J. M., & Guskey, T. R., *Implementing Student-Led Conferences.* Copyright © 2001, Corwin Press, Inc.

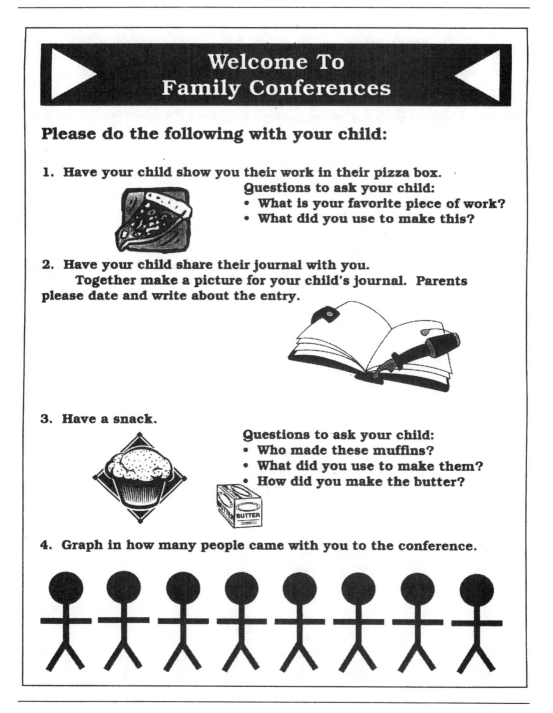

Figure 7.3. Welcome to Family Conferences

Family Conferences!

I will be doing conferences a little different this year. Your family is invited to come during the designated times to let your child show you his or her work and other things in the classroom. You will be receiving your child's Summary Report during this time. I will be available to answer your questions and concerns about your child's progress. If you feel you would like to have an individual conference with me, please feel free to contact me and we can set this up.

Conference Schedule

Choice One: Wednesday, November 11
11:00 a.m. - 7:00 p.m.

Choice Two: Thursday, November 12
11:00 a.m. - 7:00 p.m.

*Please note that a conference is mandatory. If you have a time conflict, please contact me and I will see what I can work out.

Figure 7.4. Family Conferences!

Bailey, J. M., & Guskey, T. R., *Implementing Student-Led Conferences.* Copyright © 2001, Corwin Press, Inc.

Situation 6: Non-English-Speaking Students or Parents

Teachers may need to make special accommodations during student-led conferences for students or parents whose primary language is not English. Certainly, teachers must accommodate non-English-speaking students in the classroom every day through use of special materials, visual cues, sign language, or a translator. These same accommodations must be made for parents who do not speak English.

During a student-led conference, parents and child may be able to communicate clearly using their native language. However, the teacher may be unable to communicate effectively with parents. Use of a translator may be essential so that the teacher is able to report student progress, answer questions, and help parents understand classroom expectations. Written reports to parents, too, are very important, and those may need to be in the parents' native language. When funds for hiring translators are limited, teachers have sometimes turned to high school or college students or volunteer community members to help translate information from written reports and during student-led conferences.

Final Notes

As we emphasized in previous chapters, careful and thorough preparation is the key to success for any student-led conference. Anticipating difficult situations that might occur in a school building or classroom and prevention of those situations must be part of any teacher's planning for student-led conferences. We suggest that teachers brainstorm unique situations and their solutions with colleagues. When the building principal, secretary, support staff, and teachers work together to create a plan for student-led conferences, preparation becomes much easier for the classroom teacher. Ultimately, everyone feels success.

CHAPTER 8

Evaluating Student-Led Conferences

A major reason for conducting student-led conferences is to promote student self-reflection and self-assessment. Similarly, one of the best reasons for carefully evaluating the process is to promote *teacher* self-reflection and self-assessment. Through reflection and careful evaluation, both students and teachers extend learning and improve future performances.

When we first began using student-led conferences with students from a wide variety of grade levels in several different school districts, it quickly became clear that there can be as many good models for conducting successful student-led conferences as there are creative teachers. By using some simple tools for gathering comments, teachers can learn ways to improve upon the process.

Gathering Comments From Parents

As we discussed in the Preface, thoughtful comments from parents help teachers improve the process for implementing student-led conferences. In working with hundreds of parents over the past few years, we have found that a very simple written evaluation, such as the one shown in Figure 8.1, is very effective in soliciting honest and constructive comments. Figure 8.2 shows a different format for a parent response form. Parents like to share their opinions, and they appreciate a teacher's willingness to reflect and make changes.

Some teachers hand an evaluation form to parents upon completion of the conference, ask them to take it home and return it within a week. Others ask parents to immediately spend a few minutes filling out the form while enjoying refreshments out in the hallway or in the school cafeteria. Once forms are completed, the school secretary or a classroom volunteer collects the data and assembles parent responses to questions on one page for easy review by teachers and administrators.

Parent Evaluation

Parent Name:_____
Date:_____

Dear Parents,

Thank you for participating in student-led conferences. I know this was a learning experience for all of us!

In order to make improvements, I would appreciate your thoughts on the student-led conference.

1. **What did you like about the conference?**

2. **What would you like to change?**

3. **What comments did your child have about the conference?**

4. **Do you feel you have a good picture of your child's achievement at school?**   ☐ Yes   ☐ No   **Comments:**

5. **Comments or suggestions you would like to make:**

Your comments will be very helpful to me in preparing for conferences next year. Thanks so much for your time and support!

Sincerely,

_____

Figure 8.1. Parent Evaluation

SOURCE: Adapted from work © 1995 Charlevoix-Emmet Intermediate School District

Bailey, J. M., & Guskey, T. R., *Implementing Student-Led Conferences.* Copyright © 2001, Corwin Press, Inc.

Parent Response

I came expecting . . .

I learned . . .

Student-Led Conferences

I would suggest . . .

Our comments . . .

Parent Signature:_____

Date: _____

Figure 8.2. Parent Response

Teacher observation during conferences is another way to collect good data to use in evaluating student-led conferences. For example, teachers may note the number of parents attending conferences, the number of requests for further individual conferences, and the type of questions parents ask during the conference. In addition, teachers learn a great deal about the success of conferences by watching how students and their parents interact, noting such details as how they greet each other and the teacher, what feelings are evident through facial expressions and gestures, and how long the conferences last. Finally, informal conversations with parents about the concept of student-led conferences can provide teachers with excellent suggestions for ways to improve future conferences.

Gathering Student Comments and Promoting Reflection in Class

Student comments can be some of the most insightful and helpful for improving future student-led conferences. A form such as the one in Figure 8.3 prompts older students to reflect on the entire process and offer suggestions in writing. Young children can be encouraged to draw their experiences and make written comments through the use of a form similar to Figure 8.4. One second-grade student who was asked to draw a picture of herself during conferences drew a picture of a little girl's face covered with droplets of sweat. She explained to the teacher that she was really nervous at the beginning of the conference, yet she was really glad she got to show her mom and dad what she could do. She remarked, "I learned that I don't need teachers to do things for me!"

Class discussion with students is also an effective, informal tool for evaluating the process. By taking notes on student comments, teachers can learn a great deal about the process from the students' perspective. When students become engaged in thoughtful discussion, new learning often occurs.

Gathering Comments From Colleagues

As we have worked with districts to implement student-led conferences, we have used surveys similar to the one pictured in Figure 8.5. This type of survey serves two purposes. First, it asks teachers to report quantitative data for use by administrators or others responsible for reporting on the success of student-led conferences. Second, it asks teachers to reflect on the entire process and to make suggestions for improvement.

(text continues on page 97)

▶ **After the Conference:**
Student Reflections ◀

The best thing about my conference was

Things would have gone better if

One thing I forgot to share with my parents is

One thing I chose not to share with my parents is

As I look back on my conference and the preparations for it, I feel I gained

I think my parents learned

Additional comments:

Name:_____ Date:_____

Figure 8.3. After the Conference: Student Reflections

After My Student-Led Conference

The best thing about my conference was _____
_____
_____

The thing I would change about my conference is_____
_____
_____

One thing I learned from this conference is_____
_____
_____

My parents learned _____
_____
_____

My opinion of this conference is_____
_____
_____

This is a picture of me during the conference with my parents:

Figure 8.4. After My Student-Led Conference

Bailey, J. M., & Guskey, T. R., *Implementing Student-Led Conferences*. Copyright © 2001, Corwin Press, Inc.

Teacher Survey: Student-Led Conferences

Please take a few minutes to answer the following questions. We will use this information, along with parent and student comments, to evaluate student-led conferences. We will also share all suggestions for improvements for future conferences. Thank you!

Return to: _____ by (date):_____

Name: **Grade Level or Subject:**

1. How many total students are in your class or classes?_____

2. Of these, how many students' parents participated in a student-led conference? (#) _____ *
    *Please indicate the makeup of these conferences:

    (#) _____ 1 parent attended   Other (describe situation and report #):

    (#) _____ 2 parents attended   _____

    (#) _____ "significant other" attended   _____

3. Indicate the number of parents who asked for an additional, individual conference. _____

4. Is this the first time you have tried student-led conferences as a teacher? ❑ Yes   ❑ No

5. Describe what you liked about student-led conferences.

6. Describe what you disliked about student-led conferences.

7. Would you use this process in the future? ❑ Yes   ❑ No
    If yes, what would you do differently next time?

8. Did you receive any negative comments from parents? ❑ Yes   ❑ No
    If yes, please describe briefly:

9. Describe your overall reaction to student-led conferences.

10. What additional training (if any) would help you be more effective in facilitating student-led conferences.

Use back if needed. Thank you for your comments.

Figure 8.5. Teacher Survey: Student-Led Conferences

Using a very similar survey, we were able to gather the data reported in the Preface. These data encouraged us to continue the process of student-led conferences and helped us design specific training sessions for teachers.

Additional Ways to Promote Reflection After Conferences

Two teachers we know who work as a team in a multiage classroom have used student-led conferences for several years. At the end of the conference, students give their parents the homework assignment pictured in Figure 8.6. Parents return letters in sealed envelopes by a set date. The teachers then ask students to read their letters privately and to reflect further on the student-led conference experience in writing. This activity is one that both teachers feel is very valuable for encouraging students to do their best work and for helping students build self-esteem. Parent letters and student reflection sheets are then added to the students' portfolios and often become treasured keepsakes.

Some teachers have videotaped conferences as a way to reflect on what they liked and what they would change about the student-led conference experience. Certainly, videotape should be used only with the full permission of those involved. Further, review of a videotaped performance may be intimidating to some individuals, so we caution teachers to use this method carefully. Using videotapes of family conferences for critique or discussion in a large group of students is inappropriate as this may subject individual students to embarrassment or perhaps even ridicule. Videotape review is best used with individual students only for the purpose of private reflection or discussion with a teacher. In addition, videotape can be a powerful tool for teachers to use in planning future instruction. Through listening to student comments and discussion with parents, teachers can learn what students feel is important and what they value most about their work. For example, teachers could note the amount and depth of student self-assessment and self-awareness evident during student-led conferences in order to plan future instruction for promoting growth in those areas. Used carefully and thoughtfully, videotape can provide one additional way to learn from the student-led conference experience.

Gathering Data on Student Achievement and Parent Participation

In addition to self-report survey data, teachers implementing student-led conferences should begin to collect evidence of improved student performance

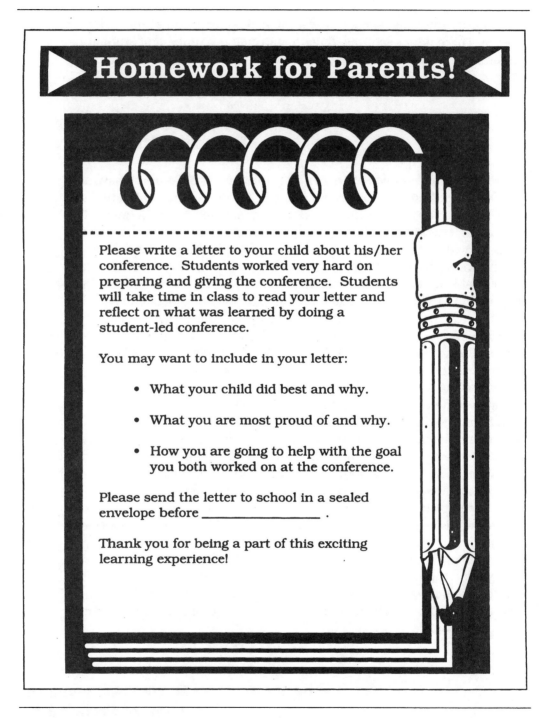

Figure 8.6. Homework for Parents!

on classroom assessments, higher quality portfolios, and higher scores on student exhibits. Although teachers may not be able to show a direct cause-and-effect relationship between student-led conferences and student performance, improved student achievement is the ultimate goal. Teachers must work together to constantly monitor student evaluation data for improvements over time.

In addition to student achievement data, many schools have chosen to collect data on the number of parents participating in student-led conferences. In many schools, increased parent participation is a building or district-wide goal, and student-led conferences are an effective way to address this goal.

With any innovation, evaluation is important. Using data gathered from parents, students, and colleagues through written surveys and formal or informal discussions, along with data on student achievement and parent participation rates, teachers can decide whether or not student-led conferences are a good addition to their system for reporting student progress. Specific feedback can also help teachers identify strengths and problems or concerns as they work to improve upon their unique model for student-led conferences.

CHAPTER 9

The Role of Student-Led Conferences in Authentic Assessment and Reporting

In Chapter 1, we discuss what we call the "3 Rs" or reasons to implement student-led conferences: (a) making student work *relevant;* (b) increasing student *responsibility* for learning; and (c) *reporting* progress on student achievement and performance to parents. In this chapter we focus on how student-led conferences can fit into any teacher's system for assessing and reporting student learning in a way that is complete and meaningful to others.

Linda Darling-Hammond (1993) cites several reasons for educators to design a system for assessing students that is authentic and rigorous. These include: (a) a concern that current tests used in the United States "do not tap many of the skills and abilities that students need to be successful in later life and schooling"; (b) a concern that the "uses of the tests have corrupted teaching practices" in that schools have begun to "teach to the test"; and (c) the knowledge that on international comparisons of student performance in mathematics and science, U.S. students "consistently score near the bottom by twelfth grade, especially on tasks requiring higher order thinking and problem solving" (pp. 19-21).

Darling-Hammond points out that there are alternatives to the type of multiple-choice, paper-and-pencil testing typically done in the United States—alternatives that challenge students by requiring them to think critically and seriously about issues, to "plan, implement and/or evaluate various tasks," or to be fully questioned by outside examiners on the "nature and quality of their thinking" (p. 23). She then asks,

> What separates these assessment strategies from the forms of testing more traditional in the United States? According to Wiggins (1989), authentic tests have four basic characteristics in common. First, they are designed to be truly representative of performance in the field. . . . Second, the criteria used in the assessment seek to evaluate "essen-

tials" of performance against well-articulated performance standards that are openly expressed to students and others . . . the third characteristic is that self-assessment plays an important role in authentic tasks. . . . Finally, the students are generally expected to present their work and defend themselves publicly and orally to ensure that their apparent mastery is genuine. (pp. 23-24)

The thoughtful work of educators such as Darling-Hammond and Wiggins coupled with our own experiences in the classroom have led us to believe that the changes in assessment practices described above are necessary and beneficial for students today. Along with changes in assessment practices, however, teachers must also make thoughtful changes to their systems for reporting student learning and progress to parents and others. Just as assessment practices need to be authentic, so do reporting practices.

Well-designed student-led conferences have the same characteristics Wiggins outlines for authentic assessment tasks. First, student-led conferences provide the opportunity for students to do the reporting, just as they might report progress to a supervisor on the job. The experience, as Wiggins (1989) notes, is "more representative of performance in the field" (p. 23). Second, through the use of carefully designed portfolios, teachers set standards that are clear and then require students to gather and provide evidence to show they have met the standards. Portfolios also promote student self-assessment, the third characteristic for authentic tasks as outlined by Wiggins. Finally, by presenting their work to parents, students are given the opportunity to "defend themselves publicly and orally" (Wiggins, 1989, p. 24). As Wiggins suggests, this oral presentation also helps students celebrate their work.

Student-led conferences are an authentic and valid means for reporting progress to parents. However, student-led conferences should not be the only method for reporting student achievement. Coupled with other measures, such as written reports, telephone conversations between teacher and parents, progress letters, or exhibitions or displays of student work, student-led conferences can round out a school's or an individual teacher's reporting system.

One first-grade teacher we know best summarizes the value and essence of student-led conferences:

My professional philosophy toward student-led conferences evolved from my interest in authentic assessment of my students. In my 21 years as a first-grade teacher, I have struggled with assessing and grading the mountain of work that goes through my classroom. Before, my students seemed to only work for a grade, smiley faces, stickers or stars. The idea of each student developing a portfolio of their best work really began to interest me. I stopped putting grades and stickers on papers. I continued to check papers while students were working, asking questions as I observed their work.

As this portfolio collection grew, it became evident that something else was needed. Sharing work. Student-led conferences became that next step. Taking the risk was terrifying and exciting. Change is hard for everyone. Student-led conferences have been well worth the effort. When done properly with lots of preparation, a teacher reaps the reward of watching students share their work, express their understanding of the work, while moms and dads beam with pride and amazement that a 6-year-old can truly lead and understand an authentic assessment conference.

Experiences like this one have brought us a long way from those ineffective and frustrating parent-teacher conferences held in the high school gymnasium as described in the Preface. Perhaps the biggest benefit of using student-led conferences is that the entire process—from planning to implementation to evaluation—provides a wonderful and rich learning experience for students, parents, and teachers. We encourage educators to look at the benefits of student-led conferences as they design assessment and reporting systems that are authentic and meaningful to all involved.

Helpful Resources for Getting Started With Student-Led Conferences

The following resources provide additional helpful ideas for teachers on how to use student-led conferences in a variety of settings.

Books

Title:	*Portfolios and Student-Led Conferencing*
Author:	Shelly A. Potter
Publisher:	The Potter Press
	P.O. Box 1803
	Birmingham, MI 48012
Copyright:	1992
Grade Level:	Elementary

Title:	*Changing the View: Student-Led Parent Conferences*
Author:	Terry Austin
Publisher:	Scholastic, Inc.
Copyright:	1994
Grade Level:	All

Title:	*Student-Led Conferencing Using Showcase Portfolios*
Authors:	Barbara Benson and Susan Barnett
Publisher:	Corwin Press, Inc.
Copyright:	1999
Grade Level:	All

Videotapes

Title:	*Student-Led Conferences*
Available From:	Charlevoix-Emmet Intermediate School District
	08568 Mercer Blvd.
	Charlevoix, MI 49720
Telephone:	231-547-9947
Copyright:	1995
Grade Level:	All
Title:	*Grading and Reporting Student Progress to Enhance Learning*
Available From:	The Video Journal of Education
	8686 South 1300 East
	Sandy, UT 84094
Telephone:	800-572-1153
Copyright:	1999
Grade Level:	All
Title:	*Student-Involved Conferences*
Authors:	Rick Stiggins and Anne Davies
Available From:	Assessment Training Institute, Inc.
	50 S.W. Second Avenue
	Suite 300
	Portland, OR 97204
Telephone:	503-228-3060
and	Classroom Connections International
	7101 Railway Avenue
	RR4, Site 430, C36,
	Courtenay, BC
	V9N 7J3
Telephone:	800-603-9888
Copyright:	1996 by Assessment Training Institute, Inc., Portland, Oregon and Classroom Connections International, Courtenay, British Columbia.
Grade Level:	All

Other

Title:	*Student-Led Conferences at the Middle Level*
Author:	Donald G. Hackmann
Format:	ERIC Digest (3 pages)
Available From:	ERIC Clearinghouse on Elementary and Early Childhood Education Champaign, Illinois
Publication Date:	1997

Title:	*School and Family Conferences in the Middle Grades*
Authors:	Rivian Bernick, Barry Rutherford, and Judi Elliott
Format:	Booklet
Available From:	U.S. Department of Education Office of Educational Research and Improvement Washington, D.C.
Publication Date:	1991

In addition to the resources listed here, educators interested in articles or other resources on the topic of student-led conferences should access the Educational Resources Information Center (ERIC) database on-line at: *http://www.askeric.org*

RESOURCE B

```
┌─────────────────────────────────────────────────────────────┐
│                                                               │
│  ▶ Before Student-Led Conferences ◀                           │
│                                                               │
│  ☐  Inform parents about the concept.                         │
│                                                               │
│  ☐  Provide staff development and support for interested teachers. │
│                                                               │
│  ☐  Work with co-curricular teachers to plan for portfolio and │
│     conference involvement.                                   │
│                                                               │
│  ☐  Talk with students about the concept and their responsibilities. │
│                                                               │
│  ☐  Set clear learning objectives for students.              │
│                                                               │
│  ☐  Work with students to create a portfolio (collection and selection). │
│                                                               │
│  ☐  Build in time for frequent reflection (for students and teachers). │
│                                                               │
│  ☐  Rehearse and role-play with students (consider videotaping). │
│                                                               │
│  ☐  Set up a committee (teachers, secretary, counselor, principal, │
│     parent, etc.) for scheduling.                            │
│                                                               │
│  ☐  Create a "family-friendly" schedule.                     │
│                                                               │
│  ☐  Attend to details such as:                                │
│        ☐  child care                                          │
│        ☐  refreshments                                        │
│        ☐  parent invitations                                  │
│        ☐  special scheduling considerations                   │
│        ☐  location (consider alternative locations such as churches, │
│           community center)                                   │
│        ☐  translators                                         │
│        ☐  special displays of student work                    │
│                                                               │
└─────────────────────────────────────────────────────────────┘
```

Figure B.1. Before Student-Led Conferences

Bailey, J. M., & Guskey, T. R., *Implementing Student-Led Conferences.* Copyright © 2001, Corwin Press, Inc.

During Student-Led Conferences

- ☐ Welcome and greet families.
- ☐ Circulate among family groups to make individual student comments.
- ☐ Observe and record:
    - ☐ pertinent student comments
    - ☐ attendance
    - ☐ questions from parents
    - ☐ family dynamics

- ☐ Write notes to students during "down time."
- ☐ Keep a list of "things to do" that come up during conferences.
- ☐ Facilitate when needed.
- ☐ Express appreciation to parents and others who attend conferences.
- ☐ Treat parents as partners.
- ☐ Provide resources or materials (such as booklets) that families can use at home to help students.

Figure B.2. During Student-Led Conferences

Bailey, J. M., & Guskey, T. R., *Implementing Student-Led Conferences.* Copyright © 2001, Corwin Press, Inc.